STO

ACPL ITEM
DISCARDED

Y0-ACG-012

JUN 6 '67

THE COMMONWEALTH AND INTERNATIONAL LIBRARY

Joint Chairmen of the Honorary Editorial Advisory Board

SIR ROBERT ROBINSON, O.M., F.R.S., LONDON

DEAN ATHELSTAN SPILHAUS, MINNESOTA

Publisher: ROBERT MAXWELL, M.C., M.P.

Rapid Revision: Commerce

FOR R.S.A., C.S.E., G.C.E. AND SIMILAR EXAMINATIONS

Rapid Revision: Commerce

BY

E. C. COLEMAN, D.P.A., F.C.C.S., F.S.C.T.
Head of Commerce Department,
Brays Grove Comprehensive School, Harlow, Essex

AND

J. B. KING, F.B.S.C.
Head of Commerce Department,
David Lister High School, Kingston-upon-Hull, Yorkshire

PERGAMON PRESS

OXFORD - LONDON - EDINBURGH - NEW YORK
TORONTO - PARIS - BRAUNSCHWEIG

Pergamon Press Ltd., Headington Hill Hall, Oxford
4 & 5 Fitzroy Square, London W.1

Pergamon Press (Scotland) Ltd., 2 & 3 Teviot Place Edinburgh 1

Pergamon Press Inc., 44–01 21st Street, Long Island City, New York 11101

Pergamon of Canada Ltd., 6 Adelaide Street East, Toronto, Ontario

Pergamon Press S.A.R.L., 24 rue des Écoles, Paris 5e

Friedr, Vieweg & Sohn Verlag, Postfach 185, 33 Braunschweig, West Germany

Copyright © 1966 Pergamon Press Ltd.

First edition 1966

Library of Congress Catalog Card No. 66–16877

Printed in Great Britain by Bradley and Son Ltd. at The Crown Press, Reading

This book is sold subject to the condition
that it shall not, by way of trade, be lent,
resold, hired out, or otherwise disposed
of without the publisher's consent,
in any form of binding or cover
other than that in which
it is published.

(2624/66)

Contents

1400033

Introduction

Rapid Revision: Commerce is divided into sections, each dealing with a different chapter found in most Commerce textbooks, being based in particular on *Practical Commerce*, by J. B. King, published by Pergamon Press. In addition, sections on general knowledge, current affairs and careers have been included.

The questions usually require only one-word or shortly phrased answers and, therefore, offer an excellent rapid method of revising the Commerce syllabus for most R.S.A., C.S.E., and G.C.E. examinations.

The book may be used in a number of ways at the discretion of the individual teacher. For example, as each chapter is completed in the textbook, the student's understanding may be tested by asking him to answer the relevant set of questions in *Rapid Revision: Commerce*. In this way, the student can tackle a wide range of questions in a very short time. This method provides a more efficient diagnostic check on the student's knowledge of the subject than an essay written on only one aspect of the chapter.

When teachers are working through a lengthy syllabus, it is often difficult to ensure that scholars have not forgotten earlier lessons. In this respect, the speed at which this book permits revision is a great asset. While the class is delving into, say, advertising and market research, the teacher can set his students a short homework assignment on an earlier topic, perhaps retail trade. Used in this way, the book keeps work, tackled some while before, fresh in the student's mind.

It is hoped that the answers section will save teachers much marking time because students, in many cases, may be permitted to check their own work. Alternatively, the teachers can ask scholars to answer the questions orally.

Towards the end of the course, *Rapid Revision: Commerce* may be used to facilitate revision of the whole syllabus. Further, a student, testing himself with this book, can go over the whole syllabus at home and, by comparing his scores on each section, can determine in which particular field his weakness lies. He can then either use the answers in *Rapid Revision: Commerce* or refer to his textbook, notes or the reference section of the library to make good his deficiencies.

Commerce examinations necessarily involve the assimilation of a good many facts as well as thought, and this book can be used effectively to impress the essential facts upon the scholar.

For a change, the questions may be used as a quiz, with the class forming two teams and the teacher acting as question master.

The questions in this book are not intended for use as tests only but as a basis for purposeful, cheerful and rapid revision of the Commerce syllabus.

We have used this method of revision for several years and it has helped us to produce some excellent results. We hope that you too will find it beneficial.

E. C. C.
J. B. K.

PART I: QUESTIONS

1. What Is Commerce?

1. Describe briefly what you understand by Commerce.
2. What have all commercial occupations in common?
3. Why are imports so vital to Great Britain?
4. How are our imports paid for?
5. How does Commerce contribute to our standard of living?
6. What are the leading divisions of Commerce?
7. Why is it important for Commerce to flourish on an international scale?
8. How can a study of Commerce benefit students?
9. What are the three broad climatic divisions of the world?
10. List the leading products we associate with each of these climatic divisions.
11. What is meant by division of labour?
12. What production advantages are derived from a system of specialization?
13. When did the Industrial Revolution begin?
14. What caused the Industrial Revolution?
15. Where is specialization most apparent?
16. How do we benefit from a division of labour?
17. List three advantages resulting from a division of labour.
18. List three disadvantages of a division of labour.
19. Give three good reasons why areas or countries specialize.
20. Give one drawback to a country specializing in one product only.
21. Mention an important item in which each of the following areas specialize: (a) Assam, (b) Ghana, (c) Iceland, (d) Denmark, (e) London.

22. Say which countries or areas specialize in the following commodities: (a) bauxite, (b) whisky, (c) dairy products, (d) port wine, (e) hardwoods.

23. In which class of work are most workers engaged in this country?

24. In which category is the next highest number employed?

25. Farmers are specialists. How many farmers are there in Great Britain? How many belong to the Agricultural Co-operative Associations?

26. What is meant by the term "production"?

27. What are the three broad divisions of productive occupations?

28. Name three different types of industry.

29. Name six direct-service occupations.

30. What is barter?

31. What were the disadvantages of a barter system?

32. What system of payment replaced barter?

33. What are the essential features of a satisfactory money form?

2. Production and Our Occupations

1. Occupations can be classified under three main headings What are they?
2. List the three leading extractive industries.
3. Give examples of three constructive industries.
4. What, briefly, is Commerce concerned with?
5. Why are some services called "direct services", and what is the essential difference between them and, say, manufacturing?
6. List four geographical factors which affect the occupations of an area.
7. Name four important ways in which occupations are affected by government legislation.
8. Into which class of occupations would you place "forestry" and what is the term for the replanting of trees on a large scale?
9. Where is the biggest fishing area around Britain, and why is it there?
10. Give a phrase (two words) for the products of the extractive industries.
11. Where is Billingsgate, and why is it there?
12. What was the leading form of transport for the early products of the Industrial Revolution, and who runs the system now?
13. Name two forms of government intervention which help to protect occupations in the United Kingdom against foreign competition.
14. List five commodities that are mined.
15. What type of environment (land, etc.) is required for hydro-electric installations, and where is such land found in the United Kingdom?

16. Which fuel provides an important industry (extractive) for Ireland?

17. Name one way in which the Government helps our international trade.

18. Why are most steel-workers employed in the Midlands?

19. What do we export, mainly?

20. What do we import, mainly? Why?

21. How would you classify "quarrying"? Name two things quarried.

22. What type of climate produces (a) softwoods; (b) hardwoods?

23. Why are most of our fishing ports in the eastern part of the country?

24. Why is a good deal of wool still produced in Yorkshire?

25. What do manufacturing industries do mainly? They convert . . . into . . . .

26. What political action by Iceland affects our fishing industry?

27. What European association is most likely to affect our trade?

28. What is meant by production?

29. Name the four essential factors required for production.

30. Give another word for "factors" of production.

31. Production usually involves changing . . . into . . . .

32. Name two things, other than land, covered by the term "land".

33. Give a more usual name for the organizer of a business.

34. What is the name given to a man who trades alone (i.e. he alone runs his business)?

35. What does our standard of living depend upon, primarily?

36. Which items are added together to give an estimate of national income?

37. What do we call the professions or services which are productive but which do not actually make commodities?

38. Can we call commercial and direct service workers productive?

39. What is the final aim of our production?

4

40. What is the Government's main machinery for sharing our national production "fruits" more evenly amongst all types of workers?

41. Does money itself *produce* any commodities?

42. Where is most of our granite quarried? (Name the town at the centre of the granite area.)

43. Is air used in the making of any products? If so, give two examples.

44. How many people, approximately, are in paid employment in the United Kingdom?

45. What is the proportion of men workers to women workers?

46. When did the Industrial Revolution begin, and end?

47. What does the word "technical" bring immediately to mind?

48. Name two important commodities produced in Ireland.

49. What name do we give to the State in which vital services (medical, pensions, etc.) are freely or cheaply available to everyone?

3. Branches of Commerce: Home Trade

1. Our trade can be divided into two broad classes. What are they?
2. Trade within this country can be classified under two headings—selling to other businesses and selling to the public: name the two.
3. Give five advantages of the wholesale system.
4. Name two commodities dealt with in wholesale which may not pass through the wholesaler's warehouse nor be handled by him.
5. Name three well-known wholesale food markets in London and say what they specialize in.
6. Wholesalers normally supply goods to retailers. Where else might the wholesaler send commodities? (Name two other recipients.)
7. List four sources of supply for goods or raw materials to wholesalers.
8. From where does the wholesaler purchase finished goods? (Name two sources.)
9. What is trade discount?
10. What is cash discount?
11. Which of the above discounts is the more important to the retailer, and why?
12. Name three headings under which one could compare a co-operative society with a multiple store.
13. What are the advantages of self-service shopping?
14. What, if any, are the disadvantages of self-service shopping?
15. Name six distinct types of retail business.
16. Why is it that multiple stores can offer goods to the public at prices lower than those of the small trader?

17. What are sole traders doing to overcome the competition provided by the larger multiple organizations?
18. If you were setting up a business as a retail grocer, where would the best position be for your shop?
19. Why are sole traders still popular today despite the competition offered by the larger organizations such as departmental stores and multiple shops?
20. What advantages does a department store offer the customer?
21. How is it that a retail market can often offer goods at lower prices than other retail units?
22. What disadvantages are there in shopping in a retail market?
23. What are the advantages of buying from a shop as opposed to a stall in a retail market?
24. What do you think is the main appeal of the co-operative societies?
25. Who founded the co-operative societies?
26. How much did each person contribute towards the first society?
27. How much must each member contribute now?
28. What was the object of the founders when they started the first co-operative society?
29. Why have some retail co-operative societies shown losses in recent years?
30. What are the advantages of the co-operative committee system of organization?
31. What are the disadvantages of the co-operative committee system of organization?
32. What are the advantages of the mail-order system of retailing to the consumer?
33. Why is the mail-order system of retailing so popular today?
34. What is a supermarket?
35. List three types of retailing *not* carried out from *shops*.
36. A producer produces something. What is the name for the customer of a retail business?
37. Need a sole trader own only one shop or type of business?
38. Which form of retail business depends almost entirely upon advertising for its customers?

4. Branches of Commerce: Foreign Trade

1. Why is foreign trade so important to Great Britain?
2. How do we pay for imports of goods from abroad?
3. What is meant by the term "balance of trade"?
4. What is meant by the term "balance of payments"?
5. For what types of goods are we renowned in the export trade?
6. What commodities do we most need to import?
7. Do our exports, in fact, pay for our imports?
8. What are invisible exports?
9. What is meant by the term "entrepôt trade"?
10. What method of transport is used to carry the bulk of the world's trade?
11. Why do we need customs officers?
12. Why do we need excise officers?
13. What are tariffs?
14. What are import quotas?
15. What functions do import duties perform?
16. If the Government should wish to protect a new U.K. industry it could use several methods. Name two of them.
17. What are the advantages, from the Government's point of view, of an import duty over an import quota?
18. What disadvantages are there in a policy of protection for British industries?
19. Briefly, why did Britain wish to join the Common Market?
20. Which other trading group did Britain join?
21. Why did the Commonwealth not wish us to join the Common Market?
22. What are the three main functions of a bill of lading?

23. What advantage does a foreign bill of exchange offer the exporter?

24. What is the advantage of a foreign bill of exchange to the importer?

25. What is a letter of credit?

26. What is the largest market for chartering vessels? Where is it and what is it called?

27. Name three important invisible exports.

5. Branches of Commerce: Transport

1. Which *five* points will a businessman bear in mind when choosing a form of transport for his goods?
2. What are the advantages of transport by air?
3. What are the disadvantages, if any, of air transport?
4. Choose the most suitable of the following words to fill in the gaps below: *small, bulky, short, lengthy, cheaper, sliding scale, tapered scale, monopoly, biased, independent, "what the traffic will bear", expensive, higher.*

    Railways in this country provide a comparatively . . . service for small consignments over short distances but a cheap form of transport for . . . consignments over . . . journeys. The longer the journey the . . . the rate per mile per ton. Such a scale of charges is known as a . . .

    Rail fares are fixed by an . . . tribunal because British Rail have a . . . of rail transport in this country. Rail fares are based on . . . Expensive, finished products are carried at a . . . rate than crude, raw materials.
5. Under what circumstances might it be against a person's interests to send goods by rail?
6. Which goods are commonly sent by passenger train, and why?
7. What caused the demise of the extensive and successful canal system of the Industrial Revolution?
8. Name two important disadvantages of canal transport.
9. Why is a liner so called?
10. What is a tramp steamer?
11. What is a charter-party?
12. What is the function of a shipping broker?
13. Where is the world's largest market for shipping of freight on a charter basis?

14. What goods are carried most commonly by coaster? On which coast of Britain is the coaster trade most brisk?

15. What are the advantages to be derived from the use of road transport for a small consignment over moderate distances?

16. Are road haulage operators' charges regulated by independent tribunals as are the railways' charges?

17. Do road haulage firms charge " according to what the traffic will bear" as do the canal and railway authorities?

18. Who does determine the cost of freight on road haulage?

19. Why is road haulage generally cheaper than rail for medium-sized consignments?

20. What are the leading advantages of choosing road transport against other methods?

21. Do you expect to see great increases in the amount of goods carried by road? Why?

22. Canals offer cheap/expensive transport.

23. What goods are commonly carried by barge within Great Britain?

24. Which is Britain's most famous canal?

11

6. Branches of Commerce: Insurance

1. What was the name of the coffee house, opened in 1680, which soon became the centre of shipping intelligence and an insurance market?

2. What is the name of the publication which deals with all kinds of shipping intelligence obtained from all parts of the world?

3. What are "syndicates" at Lloyd's?

4. What is the function of an insurance broker?

5. What is the distinction between assurance and insurance?

6. What was the purpose of fire-marks?

7. What are the three principles upon which all insurance contracts are based?

8. Explain what is meant by the term "utmost good faith".

9. Explain what is meant by the term "insurable interest".

10. Explain what is meant by the term "indemnity".

11. What is the difference between an endowment policy and a whole-life policy?

12. What is meant by the phrase "with profits policy"?

13. Select from the following words to fill the gaps below: *insurance broker, policy, insurance certificate, proposal form, premium, cover note, bank manager, syndicate, claim.*

You can obtain advice on which insurer to place your business with from an . . . You must then complete a . . . and send it, together with the necessary . . . , to the insurers. Later the broker or agent will send you an . . . which will serve as proof that you are insured. An insurance . . . provides written evidence of the exact details of the contract between the insurers and the insured. If you should be unfortunate enough to have an accident, you would make a . . . for reimbursement.

14. Explain what is meant by "loss of profits" insurance.

15. Which risks are not insurable?

16. Why is this?

17. What is an Act of God?

18. Can one insure against damage resulting from Acts of God?

19. Give two reasons why insurance is important in the export trade.

20. When does Social Insurance date from? Who introduced it?

21. Name three money benefits which people may receive from National Insurance.

22. What are the regular payments made for insurance called?

23. Name the legal document drawn up for all insurances.

24. Which type of insurance company does not have shareholders —i.e. it is not a limited company?

25. Quote a phrase which describes basically what insurance is.

26. What do insurance companies do with their "spare" money?

27. Which type of insurance must be taken out by every road vehicle driver?

28. By which type of insurance do companies insure against theft by cashiers, accounts staff, etc.?

29. In insurance, the higher the . . . , the higher the . . . (Supply the missing words.)

30. Since when, approximately, have marine insurance companies existed?

31. List three important items covered by marine insurance.

32. Is "Lloyd's of London" an insurance company? If not, what is it?

33. Who are the people at Lloyd's who carry the insurance risks?

34. Which people at Lloyd's deal directly with persons who wish to insure something or someone?

35. Is Lloyd's concerned only with marine insurance? If not, name two other types of insurance which they undertake.

36. Name two books or publications at Lloyd's which provide "marine intelligence". One of them also usually appears elsewhere. Where?

37. How many times is the Lutine Bell rung for good news and how many times for bad news?

38. Give an example of the classification of a ship at Lloyd's.

39. On which document do Lloyd's people indicate their willingness to insure the whole or part of a ship?

40. To what extent is the underwriter's liability limited?

41. How, especially, does Lloyd's contribute to Britain's export trade and to our balance of payments?

42. Who receives the net profits from a limited (insurance) company?

43. To whom do the net profits go in a mutual insurance company?

44. Name the type of policy which covers practically all risks at sea.

45. *Uberrimae fidei*—what does this mean?

46. Which country is our best insurance customer?

7. Branches of Commerce: Banking

1. From which type of merchant did the banks originate?
2. These merchants often came from Lombardy in Italy. Which London street stands on the site on which they traded?
3. List the four main types of bank.
4. Name the Big Five banks. What type of bank are they?
5. Name two types of bank account.
6. How much interest does a customer receive on his current account?
7. How much interest does a customer receive on his deposit account?
8. How much is the stamp duty on a cheque? Who finally receives the duty?
9. Why do most people today use "order" cheques in preference to "bearer" cheques?
10. List five important services provided for the public by banks.
11. What is meant by an "open cheque"?
12. Where is a cheque (a) signed, (b) endorsed?
13. What must one do about alterations made when writing cheques?
14. What is a "post-dated" cheque?
15. What is a cheque?
16. Need a cheque always be on a printed, stamp-embossed form?
17. What other form might a cheque take, if no printed form is available?
18. What is an overdraft?
19. What is the meaning of "collateral"?
20. List five ways in which banks earn money.
21. Will a bank manager divulge your balance to inquirers?

22. What is the purpose of the paying-in book?

23. What is the purpose of the bank statement?

24. Do cheques actually pass *through* the Central Clearing House today?

25. What is the function of the Central Clearing House?

26. What is the purpose of crossing a cheque?

27. What is a standing (banker's) order?

28. What is the difference between a loan and an overdraft?

29. Do banks require notice before one draws cash from a current account?

30. Do banks require notice before one draws cash from a deposit account?

31. What is a "garnishee order" in relation to a bank account?

32. What is altered on a cheque to make it a "bearer" cheque?

33. Who owns the Bank of England?

34. Give a well-known term for the Bank of England—related to other banks.

35. Who is the "payee" on a cheque?

36. Which type of cheque will not be *cashed* at a commercial bank?

37. What is the commercial bank's most useful service to Commerce?

38. Cheques are sometimes dishonoured by banks; they may be marked R/D or I/F or N.S.F. What do these marks mean?

39. A payee may endorse a cheque and pass it on to someone to whom he owes money. How do we describe the cheque then?

40. Where did the pawnbroker's sign originate? Why?

41. When was the Bank of England (a) founded, (b) nationalized?

42. Give the face values of banknotes issued by the Bank of England.

43. Name three banks set up by Charter of Incorporation (not limited companies).

44. With which Government Department is the Bank of England most closely associated?

45. What percentage of deposited money is kept in cash by the banks?

46. What happens to the money which the banks do not keep as cash?

47. How does a bank assess the charges which it makes to customers?

48. What is meant by Bank Rate? What is the present Bank Rate?

49. Can *we* become customers of the Bank of England?

50. How would Mrs. Wilhelmina Dear endorse a cheque payable to Mrs. John Dear (i.e. same person)?

51. How would J. Dunkley endorse a cheque meant for him but made payable to H. Dunkley?

52. Give two other names for commercial banks.

53. Give another name for industrial banks.

54. What is meant by (a) signing, and (b) endorsing, a cheque?

55. How can you make a cheque non-negotiable?

56. How will a bank treat a cheque presented before the inscribed date?

57. What is a negotiable instrument?

58. What is a "stale" cheque?

59. Which kind of cheque is negotiable?

60. Would a bank pay out on a cheque endorsed for and by an illiterate person as follows: John Smith X (the X is "his mark")?

61. What kind of Bank Rate is liable to make businessmen cut down on capital expenditure?

8. *Bills of Exchange*

1. Is the drawer of a bill of exchange the debtor or creditor?
2. Is the drawer of a *cheque* the debtor or creditor?
3. Which Act governs all bills of exchange?
4. Which type of bill—inland or foreign—is the most commonly used today?
5. Why is this?
6. What is a bill called before it is accepted?
7. What is it called after being accepted?
8. What is meant by the term "discounting a bill of exchange"?
9. What is a letter of hypothecation?
10. A cheque is a . . . of . . . drawn on a . . . and payable on . . .
11. What advantages do debtors derive from the use of a foreign bill of exchange?
12. What advantages do creditors derive from the use of a foreign bill of exchange?
13. What are the main differences between a cheque and a bill of exchange?
14. Where can you buy a blank inland bill of exchange?
15. How many days of grace are allowed on an inland bill of exchange?
16. What is the latest date on which the following bill of exchange can be paid: "Dated 3 April, 1966, 3 months after date"?
17. What is the stamp duty on a cheque?
18. What is the stamp duty on a bill of exchange?
19. When a bank discounts a bill of exchange, which is subsequently dishonoured, from whom are they entitled to demand payment?
20. How does a drawee "accept" a bill of exchange?

18

21. When is the drawer of a bill of exchange not the payee?

22. How can a bill of exchange be made negotiable when it is drawn up?

23. How can a bill of exchange be restricted?

24. How may one raise money on an accepted bill of exchange?

25. If you have a bill of exchange discounted, what rate per cent per annum is discounted (deducted)?

26. How is a bill of exchange a form of legal protection?

27. To whom may you sell a bill of exchange?

28. Why are bills of exchange so commonly used for overseas trade?

29. What is meant by "dishonouring" a bill of exchange?

30. What is meant by "noting" a bill of exchange, and who notes it?

31. What useful purpose is served by the noting of a bill of exchange?

9. Communications and the Post Office

1. Does the Post Office as a whole usually make a profit?

2. What is the most widely used form of communication provided by the Post Office?

3. How should one address an envelope? Draw an example of such an address.

4. In what circumstances does a telephone score over a letter as a means of communication?

5. What should one do after placing an important order by telephone?

6. What should one say first when answering a telephone?

7. Where would you look to find a person's telephone number?

8. Where would you look to find the telephone number and address of all suppliers of typewriters in your area?

9. If you could not find the telephone number of a friend of yours because your telephone directory was missing, which Post Office service could you use to obtain this number quickly?

10. What is the maximum weight for a parcel to be delivered by the Post Office?

11. If you did not know the answer to the previous question, which reference books would you consult to find the answer?

12. There are three ways in which one can arrange to send a telegram. What are they?

13. What is the minimum charge for an inland telegram of 12 words?

14. What is the cost of each additional word?

15. If no 4d. stamp has been stuck to an envelope, how much will the recipient have to pay?

16. What is the limit to the sum of money that one can draw on demand from the Post Office Savings Bank?

17. What does one do if more money is required than can be withdrawn on demand?

18. Name the various means provided by the Post Office for sending sums of money.

19. What method would you choose to send:

    (a) A crossed postal order to a mail-order company?

    (b) A Christmas present of a teddy-bear to a nephew?

    (c) A crossed cheque?

    (d) A letter which is too late to catch the usual post from London to Manchester?

    (e) An urgent message to a neighbour on holiday, informing him that his house has been burned down?

    (f) Legal documents which you must ensure have been received by the addressee?

    (g) A marriage certificate to the local council with an application for housing?

    (h) Some money urgently required by a sick relative?

20. What is the range of values for postal orders (from . . . to . . .)?

21. How can a postal order be "protected" so that it cannot be cashed?

22. May you pay a postal order into your account at (a) the Post Office; (b) your bank?

23. What is the maximum value of a money order? What else is it called?

24. What rate of interest (a) is paid by the Post Office on deposits in the Savings Bank now; (b) was paid in 1861, when the Savings Bank began?

25. How much of a person's annual interest from the Post Office Savings Bank is free of income tax?

10. Advertising and Market Research

1. What are the two basic functions of advertising?

2. What is a trade mark and why is it important?

3. Who draws up most advertising campaigns?

4. On what basis are they paid?

5. List the more common forms of advertising.

6. It has been said that advertising accounts for

> . . . per cent of the production costs of food and general household goods.

> . . . per cent of the production costs of patent foods and general toilet requisites.

> . . . per cent of the production costs of patent medicines.

> Fill in the blank percentages.

7. Advertising, by introducing consumers to the latest labour-saving devices, contributes to our rising . . . of . . .

8. Which type of retailing relies 100 per cent on advertising to make its approach to the consumer?

9. The constant repetition of the television advertising slogan probably amounts to mass . . .

10. High-pressure advertising encourages people to live . . . their . . . and to make them . . .

11. What are the leading tasks of market research organizations?

12. How do market researchers form conclusions concerning what the public wants without asking all of the public for their opinions?

13. What are the dangers of this method?

14. What form of advertising would you expect a department store to use?

22

15. What form of advertising would you expect a breakfast cereal firm to use?

16. What are the advantages of the branded-goods system to (a) the customer, and (b) the manufacturer of branded goods?

17. How can a manufacturer ensure that his branded product becomes well known? How can he protect his brand or trade mark?

ADVERTISING AND MARKET RESEARCH

15. What form of advertising would you expect a breakfast cereal firm to use?

16. What are the advantages of the branded-goods system to (a) the customer, and (b) the manufacturer of branded goods?

11. How Business Is Transacted: Documents

1. How can retailers find out all about the range of goods available?

2. What is a catalogue?

3. What is a price list? Why is it often used in conjunction with a catalogue?

4. When a retailer has decided what he will buy from a wholesaler, he will send the wholesaler an . . . If the wholesaler has these goods in stock, he will draw up at least four basic documents. These are:

    (a) An original . . .
    (b) A copy . . .
    (c) A p . . . s . . .
    (d) A d . . . n . . .

    An original invoice will be sent to the . . . and the copy invoice will be kept and given to the . . . Department. The packing slip is sent to the . . . Department so that they know what to pack and where to send the consignment. The delivery note is sent with the goods so that the retailer can . . . the consignment.

5. What is an invoice? What is its purpose?

6. What is a delivery note?

7. What would the supplier do with his copy of the invoice?

8. Normally, a supplier will send his customers a . . . of . . . at the end of the month.

9. What is a statement of account?

10. What is a credit note used for?

11. When is a debit note used?

12. What is trade discount?

13. What is cash discount?
14. Why does one have to ask specially if one wants a receipt when settling an account by cheque?
15. What is the difference between a statement and an invoice?

12. Types of Business Ownership

1. It is possible to distinguish between different forms of business organization by comparing them under three headings. What are these headings?
2. If a sole trader's business should fail, who is responsible for paying off its debts?
3. How does the sole trader obtain the necessary capital?
4. Who controls a sole trader's business?
5. How are the profits of a sole trader's business distributed?
6. What are the limits on the number of partners in an ordinary (or simple) partnership?
7. By what Act of Parliament are ordinary partnerships governed?
8. What are the four major conditions imposed by the Partnership Act if the partners have failed to draw up Articles of Partnership?
9. Who is responsible for the debts of a partnership?
10. What is a "limited partner"?
11. Do you know another name for partners who do not take an active part in running the business?
12. Can *all* partners in a business be limited partners?
13. What is limited in a limited company?
14. How does a public company obtain its capital?
15. How does a public company control the business?
16. How is the net profit of a public company distributed?
17. There are two kinds of joint stock company. What are they?
18. How many shareholders can a private company have?
19. Do both kinds of joint stock company sell shares on the Stock Exchange?
20. If the answer to question 19 is "No", which type does sell in that way?

21. To whom does the second type of company sell its shares?
22. How do co-operative societies mainly obtain the necessary capital?
23. How do co-operative societies control their business?
24. How are the net profits of co-operative societies distributed?
25. How do local government enterprises obtain capital?
26. How are local government undertakings administered?
27. How are any net profits dealt with by local government authorities?
28. How are nationalized enterprises financed?
29. Who administers nationalized enterprises?
30. How are any net profits, made by nationalized enterprises, dealt with?
31. State briefly any arguments you know in favour of nationalization.
32. State briefly any arguments you know against a policy of nationalization.
33. To what extent are the shareholders of a limited company liable financially?
34. By what word do we indicate that a limited company is "one body"?
35. Name the two types of limited company.
36. Which Act of Parliament applies to all limited companies? Give the date of this Act.
37. With whom must every limited company register? Give the full title.
38. Which two documents must a limited company register when it starts trading?
39. What main items are included in one of these documents?
40. What is included in the second document?
41. How many shareholders are permitted in a partnership?
42. How many shareholders are permitted in a private limited company?
43. How many shareholders may there be in a public limited company? If the number is limited in some way, what limits the number?

44. Which "officers" must a limited company appoint?

45. What is the attraction for a sole trader to "turn himself into a limited company" (i.e. with other shareholders)?

46. What is meant by "auditing" books, accounts, figures, etc.?

47. Which document must a public limited company send every year to the official who deals with the registration of companies?

48. What must be done annually about the books of account of a limited company?

49. Where may the public examine the registered documents and accounts of a particular limited company?

50. Why are the central records concerning limited companies open to public inspection?

51. Where must a limited company indicate the nature of its business, including what it is going to trade in?

52. Which body usually runs the affairs of a public limited company?

53. What two methods of borrowing from a bank may a company use?

54. What is the name given to the security required by a bank?

55. Which items are covered by, or included in, the Articles of Association?

56. In which type of limited company—private or public—is the capital usually the larger?

57. May a limited company sell shares beyond the value of the permitted capital?

58. Give a more usual name for the organizer of a business.

59. What is the name given to a man who trades alone (i.e. he alone organizes his business)?

60. Who supply most of the capital for the two main wholesale co-operative societies?

61. Name four important public utilities.

62. Two of these utilities are nationalized—name the utilities that are nationalized and say which other is partly nationalized.

63. Since what year has most nationalization occurred?

64. When these utilities were taken over what was given to the shareholders to compensate them?

65. Which authorities supply our water?

66. What particular advantage results from electricity being a national undertaking, as compared with when local concerns only provided electricity?

67. Which section of one of the public utilities has run at a great loss for many years?

68. What is the name of the post held by the Member of Parliament responsible to Parliament for each utility?

69. There is a central authority for each utility. Which "lesser" authority is in charge of each locality or area?

70. By what financial means is the capital raised for public utilities?

71. Would you say that the public utilities are monopolies?

72. Name four Government Departments which are directly concerned with Commerce.

73. Which nationalized institution is much controlled by the Treasury?

74. What title is given to the Minister in charge of the Board of Trade?

75. Two divisions of trade are dealt with by the Board of Trade. What are they?

13. Stock Exchanges/Stocks/Shares

1. What is a stock exchange?
2. Why is it that members of the public are not permitted in person to buy and sell securities on the floor of the exchange?
3. How many stock exchanges are there in the United Kingdom?
4. What is the function of a stockbroker?
5. What is the function of a jobber?
6. What is the general term used to describe all kinds of stocks and shares?
7. What are gilt-edged securities?
8. What is a debenture?
9. Which do debenture holders receive—interest or dividends?
10. Why are debentures a particularly safe form of investment?
11. What voting rights have debenture-holders?
12. What financial advantages, if any, do ordinary shareholders enjoy?
13. What financial disadvantages do ordinary shareholders have?
14. What rights do ordinary shareholders have?
15. In what way do preference shareholders receive preference over other shareholders?
16. Who has the first call on the profits of a company, debenture-holders or preference shareholders?
17. What advantages do cumulative preference shareholders enjoy over preference shareholders?
18. What is an "A" ordinary share?
19. "Par value" of a share—what does this mean?
20. Is there a set or usual par value for ordinary shares?
21. Shareholders receive a share of the profits if profits permit. What is this share of the profits called?

22. Through whom may the public buy the shares of a public limited company?

23. If there is no profit, do shareholders usually receive a dividend?

24. Is there a set dividend on ordinary shares?

25. In which document is the amount of the share capital shown?

26. (a) Who actually pays the interest on gilt-edged stock to the stockholder?

(b) Who really pays it (i.e. who "bears the burden")?

27. What is a share warrant?

28. Name two things that the stock exchanges deal in.

29. Which body runs the London Stock Exchange?

30. Where may *you* see lists of latest share prices?

31. How many different shares, approximately, are quoted daily in London?

32. With which persons do the public deal to buy or sell shares?

33. With which share-dealers at the Exchange do the public *not* deal?

34. What is the name for the commission or profit made by a jobber?

35. When a broker buys/sells shares for you, what does he send you that day?

36. Which document does he send you later, from the limited company, if he has bought shares for you?

37. In which book are your name and other particulars recorded by the limited company?

38. What is the term used to describe government stock?

39. Is foreign stock gilt-edged? Do the stock exchanges deal in foreign shares and stocks?

40. Name the French Stock Exchange. In which city is it?

41. In which city and street is the main U.S. Stock Exchange?

42. What is the usual face value of a preference share?

43. Can the public buy the shares of a private limited company?

44. In which document is the share capital of a limited company first recorded?

45. What mainly affects the prices of shares?

46. What is the difference between the interest on preference shares and the dividend on ordinary shares?

47. Give another name for an ordinary share.

48. On which shares is "back" interest paid, if increased profits allow?

49. Which are the more risky—preference or ordinary shares—and why?

50. By whom is a public limited company owned?

51. If shares are sold at a profit, is capital gains tax payable on such gain?

52. Is income tax payable on dividends from shares?

53. Is government tax payable on share purchases of (a) old shares, (b) new shares?

54. Where may you obtain the name and address of a stock-broker?

55. What is the motto of the Stock Exchange (in English)?

56. Can you buy co-operative society shares at the Stock Exchange?

57. Who may buy co-operative society shares—and to what value?

58. What is the "middle price" of a share?

59. What is the yield of shares (as distinct from dividend)?

60. If our foreign trade is poor, which shares are most affected? Name one type.

61. May stockbrokers advertise?

62. Are women allowed on the floor of the stock exchanges?

63. What normally is the least amount of shares that one may buy through a broker?

64. In what amounts is gilt-edged stock sold?

65. Has gilt-edged stock a fixed interest?

66. Name one of the largest investors in shares (i.e. the type of organization which invests).

67. What is it that jobbers do, as regards shares, which brokers do not usually do?

68. How much tax is charged (approximately) on the purchase of £100 of shares?

69. To which class of investor must a limited company first pay interest before it pays out any other interest or dividend on shares?

70. What is the extent of a shareholder's liability in the event of a company failing in business?

71. If you pay for only a portion of the price of a share now (5s. out of £1), how is such a share described?

72. Some speculators at the stock exchanges are known as "bulls". What is a bull?

73. Other speculators at the stock exchanges are sometimes called "bears". What is a bear?

74. Another stock exchange term is "stag". What is a stag?

14. Capital and Profits

1. Define "capital" briefly.
2. What would be the net profit of a business for 1964 if the capital at 31 December 1963 was £3000 and at the end of 1964 was £4600?
3. If at the end of 1965 the capital was £4300, what was the profit for the year ended 31 December 1965?
4. What is meant by "circulating capital"?
5. Give four examples of items included under the heading "circulating capital".
6. What is "fixed capital"?
7. Give three examples of assets which would be listed under the heading "fixed assets".
8. What is "working capital" and how is it calculated?
9. If a trader wishes to calculate his profit or loss, he simply compares his i . . . and e . . . in a certain way. He uses a . . . and . . . Account to find the profit or loss based on buying and selling alone. This profit is called his . . . profit. He uses a . . . Account to establish the final profit after the deduction of all running or . . . expenses. This final profit is known as his . . . profit.
10. On what basis is stock valued?
11. Under what circumstances can stock be shown in the Trading Account at *less* than its cost price?
12. When can stock be shown in the Trading Account at *more* than cost price?
13. What is turnover?
14. What is meant by the term "rate of turnover"?
15. What is the formula for calculating the rate of turnover?
16. How do you calculate the average stock figures?

17. What might a trader do to increase his turnover?

18. For what main purpose is capital used?

19. If income is a "*flow* of wealth", how might we describe capital?

20. What is it in a country that makes capital easy to accumulate?

21. What happens to our standard of living if fewer capital goods are produced?

22. Capital is often called " . . . labour". Supply the two missing words.

23. Which is the main organization which raises capital for limited companies?

24. Into which account do businesses place reserve money to pay for the replacement of their capital goods?

1400033

15. Saving and Borrowing Money

1. State some advantages to be derived from saving one's money.
2. What are the advantages of keeping simple accounts to record one's income, expenditure and savings?
3. After seven years a 15s. National Savings Certificate becomes worth . . . ?
4. What is the interest paid on (a) Post Office Savings Bank deposits; (b) deposit account at a commercial bank; (c) the Trustee Savings Bank?
5. What are building societies?
6. Where do building societies obtain their capital?
7. How do building societies use their capital?
8. When a man talks of taking out a mortgage, what does he mean?
9. What percentage does the Halifax Building Society pay on (a) paid up shares; (b) subscription shares?
10. What percentage does the Halifax Building Society pay on Deposit Department Accounts?
11. What advantages do Unit Trusts offer to savers, over the facilities of the Post Office Savings Bank or a building society?
12. What is a Unit Trust?
13. If you were uncertain which insurance company offered the most favourable facilities, when you wished to take out an endowment policy whom would you consult?
14. What is the essential difference between a Premium Bond and other forms of saving?
15. Which type of saving organization offers the small, short-term saver the most favourable terms and the most comprehensive facilities?

16. Which type of investment offers the most profitable means of saving to the average long-term saver?

17. In a hire-purchase transaction, the purchaser does, in fact, only . . . the goods in question, with an . . . to buy them at the end of the hire period.

18. Therefore, the goods do . . . belong to the purchaser until the l . . . instalment has been paid.

19. Under the Hire Purchase Acts, the consumer enjoys certain protections. What protection has he under these Acts?

20. What is the essential difference between hire purchase and credit sales?

21. When buying a car, what are the advantages of borrowing money from a bank over using hire-purchase facilities?

22. Why do people often prefer buying a house on a mortgage rather than renting property?

23. What is a "with profits" insurance policy?

24. One can open two kinds of credit account with a retailer. Name the two accounts.

25. What is the difference between these two accounts?

26. Name three sources from which one can borrow to buy a house.

27. If you were uncertain which of these could lend you money under the most favourable terms, whom would you consult?

28. There is only one disadvantage in dealing with a mortgage broker. What is it?

16. The Discriminating Consumer

1. Why does it pay to buy branded goods?
2. When buying a car is it worth while saving £25 on price at the expense of after-sales service?
3. Name three of the leading consumer-protection organizations.
4. With which body do you associate the "kite mark"?
5. Which magazine do you associate with the Consumers' Association?
6. Name six of the products or services tested by the C.A.
7. "Switch selling" is an example of sharp practice. What is switch selling?
8. Who pays for trading stamps?
9. Explain why.
10. What does *caveat emptor* mean?
11. What are the shortcomings of this ruling?
12. What are the main points of the Sale of Goods Act, 1893?
13. In some cases the law protects the consumer in two ways: in . . . law as a private individual and under . . . law as a member of the public.
14. Which of the following offers most benefit to the consumer: (a) rights under the Sale of Goods Act, (b) a manufacturer's guarantee?
15. If you have a reasonable complaint against a retailer or manufacturer, how can you obtain redress?
16. The consumer can obtain, under the Legal Advice Scheme, half an hour's advice from a member-solicitor for only . . . ?
17. Why should one *always* complain to the retailer and manufacturer if dissatisfied with a product?
18. Which Government Department has a "Standards Department" and why?

19. Who lays down the standards for weights and measures, and how?

20. Where may the public, in London, see a "standard yard"?

21. To what weight of water is a gallon equivalent?

22. Which councils are responsible for checking weights and measures?

23. By whom are public health inspectors appointed?

24. Mention two important matters inspected by public health inspectors.

25. To whom does a local council submit food samples for inspection?

26. By whom are factories inspectors appointed?

27. Name two important factors which are constantly checked by factories inspectors.

28. Which inspectors check conditions on farms and in slaughterhouses?

29. Is it an offence to smoke or use tobacco while handling open food intended for public consumption?

30. What sort of body is the Monopolies Commission? What standing has it?

31. Name the institution concerned with maintaining high and regular standards in manufactured goods, especially industrial goods.

32. What is the voluntary association which helps to maintain standards for the public (buyers) and which booklet does it publish monthly?

33. Give one word to indicate what it is in business which keeps up standards and so protects the customers' interests.

34. Name the two systems of paying covered by the term "deferred payments".

35. Who mostly finance these forms of instalment trading?

36. In credit sales, when do the goods become the property of the buyer?

37. If a credit sales buyer is late with his instalment, what may the seller do?

38. In credit sales, may the buyer sell the goods before he pays for them?

39. When do hire-purchase goods become the hirer's property?

40. In hire-purchase sales, what must the seller do to regain possession of some of the goods after one-third of the instalments have been paid?

41. What must the seller of hire-purchase goods indicate to the buyer (hirer) and when and how must this be done?

42. Hire Purchase Acts protect the buyer (hirer) of goods only up to certain values of goods. What is that limit?

43. Before you sign a hire-purchase agreement, what ought you to do about it?

44. Which is the cheaper method of buying—through a bank loan or through the hire-purchase system?

45. How much a year is spent on hire-purchase goods? How much approximately does this work out at for each person?

46. Is hire purchase used very much in industry and commerce? If so, why?

47. Which Government Department has most to do with hire purchase and credit sales?

48. If a prospective car-buyer wishes to check that the proposed car is not already covered by a hire-purchase agreement (and is still not paid for by the seller), where may he obtain the information?

49. What, do you think, are the Merchandise Marks Acts, 1887–1953, meant to ensure?

50. What controls have been imposed by the Food and Drugs Acts upon food, drink, medicines and drugs offered for sale to the public?

17. Abbreviations

What is the full meaning of the following abbreviations?

1. a.m.
2. b/d
3. B/E
4. B/L
5. B/P
6. B/R
7. c/d
8. C.I.F.
9. F.O.B.
10. Ex works
11. F.O.R.
12. E. and O.E.
13. e.g.
14. etc.
15. IOU
16. Ltd.
17. p.m.
18. P/N
19. pro forma

20. S.S.
21. R/D
22. C.N.
23. D.N.
24. a/c
25. C.O.D.
26. f.a.s.
27. ult.
28. inst.
29. O.H.M.S.
30. re
31. B/S
32. C. and F.
33. D/A
34. E.C.G.D.
35. L/C
36. L/H
37. W.B.

18. Sales Representatives, Agents and Markets

1. What is meant by a "free-lance" sales representative?
2. An agent sells for the owner. Give another word for owner in this case.
3. What is the distinguishing point about a factor?
4. What is the usual difference between a factor and a broker?
5. List three well-known kinds of broker.
6. Give an example of a factor in business (i.e. his trade).
7. To whom does an auctioneer sell the goods—i.e. who is the buyer?
8. List three types of expensive goods sold by specialist auctioneers.
9. Name two well-known London auctioneers (i.e. the company names).
10. Through which agent abroad do merchants often sell goods, for safety?
11. What is the main advantage of appointing the agent named in question 10?
12. Where is the main market for government stock? Name the stock, too.
13. Name two important commodities sold in New Zealand wholesale markets, for export in particular.
14. Some of the fish sold at Billingsgate is sold by auction and the remainder by private treaty. Which deliveries of fish are sold by auction, and what type of auction system is used?
15. Which Government Department is most concerned with the fishing industry?
16. Which body exists solely for dealing with the herring industry? Where are its offices?

17. Name a very important body to which the Prime Minister usually appoints a member to represent the fishing and agriculture industries.

18. Do you know how many millions of hundredweights of fish, approximately, are landed each year by our fishermen?

19. What proportion of the catch is caught by (a) England and Wales, (b) Scotland?

20. How many men in our fishing industry are employed in catching fish?

21. Which invention enables fish to be kept fresh over long distances? After what date did this invention begin to play an important part in long-distance transport?

22. Fish at Billingsgate is sold by two types of seller. Name them.

23. If our fishermen catch a sturgeon, what happens to it?

24. What famous delicacy is made from part of the sturgeon?

25. We are the world's second-largest catchers of fish. Which country catches more fish than we do?

26. What are the two main points about a "perfect market"?

27. What is imperfect in an "imperfect market"?

28. Which system provides a very expensive, restricted market for some goods?

29. Which national body (a court) exists to try to ensure that individuals or companies do not wrongly dominate any market?

30. What has caused many markets to spread—even become worldwide markets, instead of purely local affairs?

31. Which market includes banks, finance houses, merchant bankers and other financial institutions?

32. Where is the main market for gilt-edged stock?

33. Name the London wholesale markets for fish, meat and vegetables.

34. Which agents represent most producers of tea, coffee, cocoa, spices and similar commodities?

35. Is the London Stock Exchange a near-perfect market or an imperfect one?

36. What is the old name, but still used, for a market-place or building where corn, cotton or wool (for example) is bought and sold?

37. Which area or street in London is renowned as the market for precious stones and jewels?

19. General Knowledge: Transport and Inventions

1. From what time in particular have inventions played a very important part in industry and commerce? Give an approximate date and name the period.
2. When were public steam railways started, and where?
3. When, approximately, were steam-ships first used?
4. When was refrigeration for ships invented/introduced?
5. In which decade were motor-cars first used?
6. When was the first aeroplane flight—and where?
7. Name two other flying-machines, developed from aeroplanes.
8. Name two systems of writing, by hand, other than ordinary writing.
9. Name two important medical inventions (a) to check the heart beat, (b) to photograph parts inside the body.
10. Name two ways in which inventions have reduced man's work.
11. Which *group* of inventions has most affected the location of industry?
12. Name three inventions which have helped to increase/improve agricultural production.
13. Name two inventions, used in offices, which have speeded communications.
14. Name three man-made materials which have benefited men and women.
15. What power drives a hydro-electric installation? Where are most of such installations in the United Kingdom?

16. Name three kinds of power (fuel) which drive mechanical road vehicles.
17. Name a system of working which was devised in the eighteenth century to improve and increase the output of crops.
18. Inventions have led to increased division of labour. Give one word for this division.
19. How are inventions protected—and through which Government Department?
20. Which fairly recent invention helps to safeguard the movement of ships and aircraft?
21. Name two inventions which are important in preserving food.
22. What system was "invented" for safeguarding milk? By whom?
23. Which important invention revolutionized road transport in the 1890's?
24. Who invented wireless telegraphy? When?
25. When was television invented? By whom?
26. Graham Bell invented something. What? When? Where?
27. Which authorities are responsible for most of our public transport?
28. During what period did canals increase and prosper?
29. Name three commodities carried by tankers (ships).
30. Which stationary equipment can be used to transport certain commodities, notably liquids?
31. Name three of the commodities referred to in question 30.
32. When was margarine invented? Where?
33. Why is margarine so called?
34. Who discovered penicillin?
35. When was the first typewriter invented?
36. When was Terylene first made in Britain?

20. General Knowledge: Food Production and Distribution

1. What proportion of our food is produced in the United Kingdom?
2. Originally margarine was made from beef-fat. Now, most of it consists of vegetable oils. Can you name two trees/plants from which the oils come?
3. From which grain are corn flakes made—and where is most of such grain grown?
4. Which invention for nearly 100 years has most helped in the preservation of perishable goods in transportation?
5. From which vegetable is home-produced sugar obtained?
6. What is the name for the payment made to farmers by the Government to encourage farmers to maintain or increase production of certain crops or livestock, often in the face of foreign competition?
7. Which crop, connected with beer, is now mostly gathered by machine instead of by hand by families from the East End of London?
8. Name two ways of preserving foods other than by refrigeration.
9. On which imported foods does the United Kingdom usually spend most money in a year? Name two.
10. Which councils are responsible for checking the quality, purity and content of food and drink on sale to the public?
11. To whom do these councils submit for analysis the samples obtained by their inspectors?
12. Approximately twice as many turnips and swedes as potatoes (by weight) are generally grown each year in the United Kingdom—approximately 10,000,000 tons. Why?

13. If there is a shortage of beef in the shops, what is likely to happen to the price?

14. And what will happen to the prices of substitutes (other meats or fish) if beef prices rise and less beef is bought?

15. Which councils are responsible for checking the weights and measures used in the sale of food and drink?

16. Which country produces most of the world's cocoa?

17. Of the many foods which we import from Australia, name three on which we spend most in any year.

18. Which country is the world's greatest importer of foods?

19. Name three large wholesale food markets in London.

20. The Ministry of Agriculture, Fisheries and Food is responsible for schemes operated by Boards for the marketing of particular foods on behalf of the producers or for advising on marketing. Can you name two such Boards?

21. Which sign is stamped on eggs by the appropriate Board?

22. How many farmers are there, approximately, in the United Kingdom?

23. For which drinks are the following places famous: (a) Somerset, (b) Scotland, (c) Burton-on-Trent, (d) Ireland?

24. What are "tin-cans" made of?

25. Which dried fish are forms of herrings?

26. To which countries do we export large quantities of fish? Why?

27. Which South American country sells us large quantities of corned beef?

28. What is the substance used to lighten (to aerate) bread and beer?

29. How many pounds to a stone of fish?

30. Which fish is said to bear the imprint of Jesus's thumb and index finger?

21. General Knowledge: Population

1. What, approximately, is the population of the United Kingdom?
2. Over the past 100 years, food supplies in this country have increased enormously. Mention two reasons for this.
3. What is an optimum population?
4. Has Japan an optimum population?
5. Has Australia an optimum population?
6. What was the population of the United Kingdom in 1801, at the first census?
7. Are there more women than men in the United Kingdom? If so, how many more?
8. Ours is an ageing population—how many people are over 70 years of age?
9. How many of our population are in paid work?
10. Approximately, how many men and how many women have paid jobs?
11. Which industries employ most people?
12. Which industry employs the next highest number of people?
13. Have we room and work in the United Kingdom for thousands more immigrants from Commonwealth countries?
14. To which country do most emigrants go from the United Kingdom?
15. What two main effects does an ageing population have on the people at work?
16. Do similar effects result from young people staying longer at schools, colleges and universities?
17. The population of London (1964) was about 8,000,000. Can you name two countries with an entire population no greater than that of London?

18. Give two good reasons why there are many fewer farm-workers than there were 100 years ago.

19. Why are there comparatively few people in northern Scotland?

20. Could we maintain our standard of living if we depended solely on the food and other commodities produced by our own population?

21. Give one good reason why people retire earlier and live longer than previously.

22. Which international organization is studying farming problems in many lands in order to try to increase output?

23. The density of population in the United Kingdom is about 600 persons per square mile. Would you say that this is one of the highest in the world?

24. In which two classes of occupations is the number of workers steadily increasing?

25. Why is this so?

26. In which of the following areas is the unemployment rate highest: England, Scotland, Wales, Northern Ireland?

27. Have you any idea what percentage of the working-age population is unemployed at any one time?

22. Careers in Commerce

MAINLY FOR GIRLS

The Office Junior

1. What duties would you expect an office junior to perform?
2. How much would you expect her to earn?
3. What training and qualifications do you think she would require?
4. What prospects might the average office junior expect?

The Copy Typist

1. What duties would you expect a copy typist to perform?
2. What salary would you expect her to earn at 16 and at 25?
3. What training and qualifications would she require?
4. What prospects might the average copy typist expect?

The Comptometer Operator

1. What does the work of a comptometer operator entail?
2. What salary would you expect her to earn at 16 and at 25?
3. What training and qualifications would she require?
4. What prospects might the average comptometer operator look forward to?

The Telephonist

1. What does the work of a telephonist entail?
2. What salary would you expect her to earn at 16 and at 25?
3. What training and qualifications would she require?
4. What prospects might the average telephonist expect?

The Audio-typist

1. What work does an audio-typist perform?
2. What salary would you expect her to earn at 16 and at 25?
3. What training and qualifications would she require?
4. What prospects might the average audio-typist expect?

The Shorthand-typist

1. What work does the average shorthand-typist perform?
2. What salary would you expect her to earn at 16 and at 25?
3. What training and qualifications would she require?
4. What prospects might the average shorthand-typist expect?

The Private Secretary

1. What work does the average secretary perform?
2. What salary would you expect her to earn at 18 and at 25?
3. What training and qualifications would she require?
4. What prospects might the average secretary expect?

The Medical Secretary

1. What work does the medical secretary perform?
2. What salary would you expect her to earn at 19 and at 25?
3. What training and qualifications would she require?
4. What prospects might the average medical secretary expect?

The Punch-machine Operator

1. What work does the punch-machine operator perform?
2. What salary might a punch-machine operator expect to earn at 16 and at 25?
3. What training and qualifications would she require?
4. What prospects might the average punch-machine operator expect?

MAINLY FOR BOYS

The Accountant

1. What work does an accountant perform?
2. What salary might a trainee accountant command at 18?
3. What training and qualifications are required?
4. What are the prospects for the average qualified accountant?

The Clerical Officer: Civil Service

1. What sort of work would a clerical officer perform?
2. What salary might a clerical officer earn at 16 and at 25?
3. What training and qualifications are required?
4. What are the prospects for a clerical officer?

The Executive Officer: Civil Service

1. What sort of work would an executive officer perform?
2. What salary might an executive officer receive at 16 and at 25?
3. What training and qualifications are required?
4. What are the prospects for an executive officer?

Customs and Excise Officers

1. What sort of work do customs and excise officers perform?
2. What salary might a customs officer earn at 16 and at 25?
3. What training and qualifications are required?
4. What are the prospects for a customs or excise officer?

The Company Secretary

1. What sort of duties would a company secretary perform?
2. What salary might a company secretary command?
3. What training and qualifications are required?
4. What are the prospects for a company secretary?

The Bank Clerk

1. What sort of duties would a bank clerk perform?
2. What salary would a bank clerk receive at 16 and at 25?
3. What training and qualifications are required?
4. What are the prospects for a bank clerk?

The Insurance Clerk

1. What sort of duties would an insurance clerk perform?
2. What salary would an insurance clerk receive at 16 and at 25?
3. What training and qualifications are required?
4. What are the prospects for an insurance clerk?

PART II: ANSWERS

1. *What Is Commerce?*

1. Commerce provides a "chain" of services to bridge the gap which separates industry from the consumer. Commerce makes it possible to market the produce of industry on the one hand and supplies the consumer with the goods he requires on the other. The five major links in the chain of Commerce are:

> Trade
> Transport
> Banking
> Insurance
> Advertising.

2. All commercial occupations play some part in making possible the distribution of goods to the consumers who need them.

3. (a) We live on a small island and have a large population. (Every square mile of Great Britain supports about 559 people. This density of population is eleven times that of the average for the rest of the world.) Therefore, there is insufficient arable and grazing land available to provide sufficient food for our population. (Approximately 50 per cent of our food is home-produced. The rest has to be imported.) Although Britain is such a small island, we are the world's largest importers of cereals. We are, therefore, dependent upon vital imports of food to provide us with about 50 per cent of our food requirements.

(b) Our vital imports have to be paid for. We earn most of the necessary purchasing power by exporting a wide variety of manufactured goods. In addition to our need for imported food, our manufacturing industries are now so large that they need to *import* vast quantities of raw materials in order to produce more goods for *export*.

We therefore need to import food in order to survive and we have to import most of our raw materials before we can begin to manufacture goods with which to pay for our imports.

4. Our imports are paid for with earnings from exports of goods and "invisible" exports.

5. (a) Commerce organizes the complex system of imports and exports so vital to our very survival.

(b) The various branches of Commerce arrange for the produce of the world to be brought to our locality so that we have the choice of a wide variety of foodstuffs and exotic fruits, etc. Commerce also makes possible the distribution of luxuries and labour-saving devices such as television sets, refrigerators, washing-machines, scooters and cars.

(c) The world of Commerce provides employment for a large sector of our population.

6. Trade, transport, banking, insurance and advertising.

7. Few countries are completely self-supporting, due largely to variations in climatic conditions, raw materials available, the skill of the local labour-force, etc. Such nations require goods and services to be supplied by other nations. For these reasons the nations of the world are said to be interdependent, and if the needs of these countries are to be satisfied, Commerce must organize the necessary trade between them.

8. A study of Commerce is particularly valuable to those who wish to make their careers in Commerce. It gives them a basic understanding of the work they will be doing in relation to other commercial workers and to the satisfaction of consumers' wants.

Commerce also has relevance to other scholars, no matter what trade or profession they are planning to enter, since it is so closely related to the complex economies of everyday life in the twentieth century.

Further, if students can pass a C.S.E., R.S.A., or G.C.E.

examination in Commerce, they will have a valuable qualification, which will also be of practical use to them in their chosen careers.

9. Cold, temperate and hot.

10. Cold: fish, whale oils and soft timber.

Temperate: cereals, dairy produce and timber. In this zone are also found the leading industrial nations.

Hot: tropical fruits, oils, rubber and hardwood.

11. Specialization.

12. People who specialize become expert at their work. They do jobs more quickly, more efficiently and more cheaply than non-specialists.

13. The Industrial Revolution began about 1760.

14. Inventions which enabled mechanical power to be applied to tools and other productive equipment (e.g. in the cotton mills).

15. In industry and Commerce and particularly in mass-production factories.

16. We enjoy cheaper goods and a higher standard of living.

17. *Examples:*
(a) Greater dexterity and speed made possible, resulting in higher production rates.
(b) Mass-production, resulting in lower prices.
(c) Machines save much heavy labour by hand.
(d) Time saved in training.
(e) Allows more workers to engage in producing more luxury and capital goods.
(f) Mass-production techniques make it possible for people to have shorter working weeks and more leisure time and make more time and money available for education.

18. *Examples:*
(a) Monotony.
(b) Loss of craft.
(c) Labour tends to become immobile (unwilling to move elsewhere).
(d) The absence of a "key" man may hold up production.

57

(e) The absence of one component may bring a complete assembly-line to a standstill.

19. (a) Because of a need to exchange products for more urgent commodities (e.g. the United Kingdom exchanges manufactured goods for food and raw materials).

(b) Natural resources, climate, position in the world, nature of the land, local skills.

20. *Examples:* danger of economic collapse if fashion or tastes change. In wartime it may not be possible to exchange goods and the country would have only one main product. Another country might produce a similar item or a synthetic product and win the market by selling at lower prices.

21. Assam: tea.

Ghana: cocoa and gold.

Iceland: fish and cod-liver oil.

Denmark: dairy products.

London: Commerce (all branches) and industry (mixed).

22. Bauxite: Jamaica and U.S.A.

Whisky: Scotland and Ireland.

Dairy Products: most temperate zone countries or areas, e.g. Denmark, New Zealand, Australia.

Port Wine: Oporto in Portugal.

Hardwoods: equatorial forest areas, e.g. Central Africa, Amazon jungle, Burma and South-East Asia.

23. Manufacturing industries.

24. Commerce.

25. Approximately 300,000 people are farmers. Of these about 200,000 belong to the Agricultural Co-operative Associations (i.e. 2 out of every 3 farmers are members).

26. The satisfaction of the wants of consumers.

27. Industry, Commerce and direct services.

28. Extractive, manufacturing and constructive.

29. *Examples:* doctors, dentists, teachers, lawyers, solicitors, policemen, actors.

30. Barter is the system of trading whereby goods are exchanged directly for other goods, using no money.

31. All trade was dependent upon a "coincidence of wants" (if a cobbler wanted to exchange a pair of shoes for a cloak, he had to find a tailor with a cloak to dispose of *who wanted* a pair of shoes).

Where perishable goods were concerned it was difficult to store wealth.

Goods used for barter were difficult to value in terms of other articles, and often impossible to break down into low values (e.g. if it was decided that a sheep was worth six smocks, what was a farmer to do when he only required one smock? He could have cut the sheep into six parts and paid with one portion. But then, mutton would not keep for very long and the remaining five-sixths of a dead sheep would not have been of much use to him.)

32. Money was used as a "medium of exchange".

33. First, a satisfactory money form must be something that everyone wants and, therefore, values.

Secondly, it should be easily portable. It should offer great value in small bulk.

Thirdly, it should be durable.

Fourthly, it should be issued in a wide range of denominations from high to low values. In other words, it should be divisible

2. Production and Our Occupations

1. Industry, Commerce and direct services.

2. Farming, fishing and mining.

3. *Examples:* ship-building; road-making; bridge-building; building of houses, shops and factories; railway construction.

4. Trade, transport, banking, insurance and advertising.

5. They provide a personal service, e.g. doctors, dentists, nurses, lawyers, teachers, policemen, fire-officers and actors. Manufacturing produces goods, direct services do not.

6. *Examples:* climate, position in the country or world, relief, natural resources (raw materials), size of country, population and the skills of workers.

7. *Examples:* taxation (increases or decreases demand); tariffs; quotas; government aid; Social Insurance; nationalization; wages policy; provision of new towns; Education policy (more or fewer teachers, students, buildings, books, scholarships, etc.).

8. Extractive; reafforestation.

9. The Dogger Bank in the North Sea; it is shallow—plankton flourish there.

10. Raw materials.

11. On the north side of the Thames, between London Bridge and Tower Bridge. It is a wholesale fish market and is situated at Billingsgate because this point is easily reached from the sea or from land. It serves, mainly, London's great population.

12. Canals; British Inland Waterways.

13. The imposition of quotas or tariffs. Also subsidies (grants) to farmers and some other producers.

14. *Examples:* coal, ores, gold, salt, mineral oils, atomic fuels.

15. Mountainous, with fast-flowing water; Scotland and Wales mainly.

16. Peat.

17. Through British embassies, consulates, commercial agents in overseas countries; arranging for displays of British goods at trade fairs, here and abroad; sending trade delegations abroad; export credit guarantees—a form of insurance.

18. The manufacturing industries grew up around the Midlands area because the materials for steel-making (ore, coal and limestone) were originally mined there. Nowadays, most raw materials are imported but the Midlands remain the centre for the manufacture of steel goods due to the engineering skills of the population, born of tradition.

19. Manufactured goods, especially mechanical items (e.g. cars, machines, aircraft). A more detailed breakdown of Britain's exports is given below:

Approx.

Manufactured goods: machinery, vehicles, aircraft, textiles, iron and steel	84%
Raw materials, coke, wool and other animal hair	10%
Foodstuffs, beverages, etc., and tobacco	6%

20. Food and raw materials—because we produce only about 50 per cent of our food needs; we also require raw materials in order to make goods for export. A more detailed breakdown of Britain's imports is given below:

Approx.

Raw materials: petroleum, wood, wool, cork, cotton, metal ores and scrap	40%
Foodstuffs: cereals, meat, beverages, tobacco	40%
Manufactured goods, non-ferrous base metals, chemicals, etc.	20%

21. Extractive industry. *Examples:* chalk, slate, granite, marble, clay.

22. (a) Softwoods: temperate and cold climates; (b) hardwoods: hot climates; *some* in temperate climates.

23. Most of our fishing ports are situated on the eastern coast of Britain because these ports are accessible for the boats fishing the Dogger Bank area and northern and eastern seas, and also because they are within easy reach of the consumers in densely populated towns.

24. Excellent grasslands for sheep and water for wool-washing and dyeing. The industry still persists where it started originally, despite the fact that most of our wool is now imported (mostly from Australia and New Zealand).

25. . . . raw materials into finished products.

26. The imposition of a 12-mile fishing limit. Fishermen from the United Kingdom used to fish up to 3 miles from Iceland.

27. The Common Market.

28. Production is the provision of goods or services which satisfy the consumer's wants, e.g. growing, making, quarrying, mining, transporting, or taking any action which makes something ready—or a stage nearer readiness—for the consumer.

29. Land, labour, capital and enterprise/organization.

30. Agents (of production).

31. . . . raw materials into finished products.

32. *Examples:* raw materials, crops, fish, water, buildings, air.

33. "Entrepreneur"—in addition to organizing, this term implies a degree of risk-bearing.

34. Sole trader.

35. The amount of services and commodities "produced" for our consumption or to exchange for other things that we need, e.g. food, raw materials.

36. Incomes (wages/salaries), profits, rents, interest on investments.

37. Commercial and direct services.

38. Yes, they help (sometimes indirectly) to produce goods.

39. To improve, or at least maintain, our standard of living by increasing the output per head of the working population.

40. Taxation.

41. No, although the prospect of making money may tempt *people* to produce more commodities.

42. Aberdeen.

43. Yes. *Examples:* oxygen for hospitals and aircraft; for supplying pressure for spraying, pumping tyres, working brakes; for making nylon, for filling plastic balls, for drying goods (e.g. cloths, fruits).

44. About 25,000,000.

45. 2 to 1; about 17,000,000 men and boys to 8,000,000 women and girls.

46. About 1760; it has *not* ended yet, although modern industrial improvements also stem from automation, computers, atomic power, etc.

47. "Technical" relates mostly to skills in mechanical or applied arts and the word usually brings to mind such words as "machinery", "industry", "inventions", and "engineering".

48. *Examples:* linen, whisky, linseed oil, pigs, bacon and pork.

49. The Welfare State.

3. Branches of Commerce: Home Trade

1. Home trade and foreign trade.

2. Wholesale and retail trade.

3. *Examples:*
(a) Wholesalers undertake the distribution problems which otherwise the manufacturer would have to face himself.
(b) They buy the producer's goods as they become available and pay for them; this keeps the producer's business steady.
(c) They give credit to retailers.
(d) They provide storage space which the producers might not have.
(e) They provide a central warehouse where the buyer may choose from a wide selection of manufacturers' goods.
(f) They save transport for producers and retailers by distributing the goods.
(g) They keep retailers informed of latest trends in the market and bring the full range of goods to their attention (by catalogues or representatives).
(h) They keep the manufacturers informed of the buyer's needs.
(i) They tend to keep prices steady by keeping ample stocks of goods at all times.

4. *Examples:* mostly raw materials and foods (especially imported goods) which the wholesale agent or broker may sell by reputation only or by showing small samples (e.g. from a ship-load of cotton, wool or cocoa); the goods would then be delivered from the supplier, perhaps from a ship, to the buyer's premises.

5. Covent Garden/Spitalfields: fruit, vegetables, flowers.
Smithfield: meat and poultry.
Billingsgate: fish/shellfish.

6. To manufacturers (e.g. a wholesale timber merchant may sell timber to a furniture factory or match factory), and to buyers abroad.

7. *Examples:* U.K. growers, U.K. manufacturers; other wholesalers; overseas growers; overseas manufacturers; through auctions, factors, brokers and other agents.

8. From factories and from other wholesalers, at home and overseas (often through agents).

9. Trade discount is a deduction from the price of an article, allowed the purchaser by the seller. For example, the difference between the price the retailer pays for an article and what he charges the public is trade discount and constitutes his margin of profit. This profit margin is required by the retailer to enable him to pay the expenses incurred in the running of his business. One should always remember that it is upon trade discount that the trader relies to pay his expenses and to earn his livelihood.

10. Cash discount is a deduction from invoice or account allowed in order to encourage purchasers to settle their debts promptly. Generally, the quicker the invoices are paid, the larger the cash discount, e.g. a firm might allow a 5 per cent deduction for cash in 14 days and only $2\frac{1}{2}$ per cent for cash in one month.

11. Trade discount is the more important to the retailer since it is the larger of the discounts and is relied upon by traders for their profit margins.

12. (a) How the capital is obtained.

(b) How the business is administered.

(c) The basis on which profits are distributed.

13. (a) Quicker, more convenient shopping.

(b) Wider variety of goods *on display* than possible with the "counter system".

14. The methods of display and subtle sales techniques persuade many people to buy goods which they do not really

D

need and which they would never have thought to ask for in a "counter service" shop.

15. *Examples:* (a) Sole traders, (b) multiple shops, (c) department stores, (d) stalls in a retail market, (e) discount stores, (f) co-operative societies, (g) mail-order businesses, (h) direct selling, (i) travelling shops, (j) chain stores.

16. Because multiple stores buy centrally and so obtain larger trade discounts than sole traders are able to obtain with their comparatively small orders.

17. Many sole traders are forming Trade Guilds and Associations in order to be able to obtain the benefits of central buying and higher trade discounts. *Examples of guilds:* Spar, Mace, Association of Private Traders. (A number of these trade guilds arrange other services such as group advertising in newspapers, magazines and on television for a nominal membership fee.)

18. In a densely populated area, in a central position, close to car parks, and, if possible, on a corner site.

19. (a) Personal service.

(b) Sometimes allow credit.

(c) Open longer hours than larger concerns.

(d) Many sole traders provide free delivery service.

(e) Small local shops are often more handy for local house-wives.

20. (a) "One-stop" shopping made possible, since there are many departments housed under one roof.

(b) A wide variety of goods—usually of good quality.

(c) Competitive prices due to rapid turnover making possible policy of bulk-buying and large trade discounts.

21. Market stall-holders do not have to pay the high overheads that shopkeepers face.

22. (a) You are not able to try on articles of clothing.

(b) You are seldom allowed to return goods which prove unsatisfactory.

(c) It is often uncomfortable to shop in the open in winter or in bad weather, and most markets are of the open-air variety.

23. (a) More comfortable surroundings in which to make one's selection.

(b) One can try on articles of clothing in comfort and privacy.

(c) One can usually change goods which prove unsatisfactory.

24. The system of dividends on purchases.

25. The Rochdale Weavers (or "Pioneers").

26. They each paid 2d. a week until they had raised £1 each towards the necessary capital with which to open a retail grocer's shop.

27. Each member must pay 1s. entrance fee and buy at least one £1 share.

28. The object of the Rochdale Pioneers was to provide themselves with a shop of their own from which they could buy food at low prices.

29. (a) Retail Co-operative Societies no longer provide goods at lower prices than other retail shops, such as the leading multiple and cut-price shops.

(b) Further, the dividend on purchases has been reduced, and in any event the dividend idea is not as popular with most housewives as an instant cash saving.

30. Customers can have some say in the running of the shops in which they do their shopping.

31. Such committee members/customers are rarely employed in the retail trade and are not, therefore, expert in the running of a large organization as are specialists.

32. (a) Hire-purchase or credit-sale facilities are readily available for most goods sold by mail-order companies.

(b) Goods can be obtained without leaving one's home, by studying a catalogue and sending off an order by post.

(c) Prices are often competitive.

(d) Goods obtained from reputable mail-order concerns are usually of good quality.

(e) People living in areas far from shopping centres are saved much travel, expense and inconvenience by using mail-order facilities.

33. Mainly due to the availability of comprehensive hire-purchase or credit-sale facilities on a wide range of goods and clothing, but also because many housewives are at work when the shops are open.

34. A large shop with many display stands under one roof which employs a self-service method of shopping.

35. *Examples:* mail order; market stalls; door-to-door selling; newspaper selling; milk/greengroceries/bread deliveries; direct-selling, e.g. road-side farm sales.

36. A "consumer" (we consume not only food, but also clothes, shoes, furniture, motor-cars, cutlery, etc.).

37. No, he may have several, each managed by an employee

38. Mail-order businesses.

4. Branches of Commerce: Foreign Trade

1. Britain is a fairly small island with a large population. There is insufficient land from which to obtain all the food and raw materials required. Therefore, we must import food and raw materials in order to survive. Most of our imports have to be paid for by purchasing-power obtained by exporting goods.

2. We usually manage to pay for imports by exporting goods together with money earned from invisible exports.

3. The balance of trade is the relationship between our total exports and our total imports.

4. The balance of payments is the difference between our *total income* (from exports *plus* invisible exports) on the one hand and our *total expenditure* overseas on the other.

5. Engineering products, chemicals, motor-cars, railway engines and rolling stock, fertilizers, chemicals and textiles.

6. Grain, meat, raw materials.

7. Not usually. (Net income from invisible trade is also needed.)

8. Invisible exports are services rendered to overseas countries which earn us foreign currency. *Examples:* income from shipping, air freights, passenger flights, tourism, overseas investments and insurance.

9. The import of goods in order to export them again is known as "entrepôt trade".

10. Shipping.

11. Customs officers are required to see that the statutory duties have been paid on all goods imported and that import quotas are complied with.

12. Excise officers are required to see that all duties are paid on dutiable items produced in this country (e.g. tobacco, wines).

13. Tariffs are lists of imports on which customs duties are payable.

14. Import quotas stipulate the quantity of particular goods which may be imported from a specified country.

15. Import duties tend to reduce the import of goods on which they are imposed since they make the goods relatively more expensive when they reach the home market.

16. Tariffs or import quotas; subsidies.

17. Import quotas and tariffs bring about a reduction in imports, but tariffs also bring in revenue (import duties) to the exchequer whereas the system of import quotas does not.

18. With a policy of protection, British industries lose the spur of competition. Competition is healthy and keeps manufacturers on their toes, thus ensuring that the public are offered good quality goods at reasonable prices. Some industries use the protection of tariffs and quotas to cover their inefficiency and lack of enterprise.

19. So that Britain's exports to Common Market countries would not have to bear the tariffs we must pay if we remain out of the market.

20. E.F.T.A.—European Free Trade Area.

21. The Commonwealth countries did not wish Britain to join the Common Market because they feared that Britain would be forced to impose high tariffs on food imports from the Commonwealth, which would have effectively reduced the volume of trade.

22. A bill of lading is: (a) a document of title—whoever holds it has first claim on the goods; (b) an agreement between shipper and shipowner; (c) a receipt for the goods entrusted to the captain.

23. (a) The exporter can be sure that the goods will not be handed over to the importer until he has either paid or accepted the foreign bill of exchange.

(b) If the bill is a bill against acceptance (B/A) the exporter can discount it and so obtain the money due to him without waiting (minus the discounting charge made by the bank or discount house).

24. (a) The importer is not required to pay, or accept, the bill until he has seen that the goods have arrived safely and are as he ordered.

(b) If the bill is a bill against acceptance (B/A), he has a period of credit in which to sell the goods and so raise the money to pay for them when the bill becomes due.

25. A letter of credit instructs a bank to transfer a certain sum of money to an account in a foreign bank, where it may be drawn upon by the exporter as and when he satisfies his part of the bargain by forwarding goods to the importer.

26. The Baltic Exchange, situated in London.

27. *Examples:* income from shipping, airlines, tourists visiting this country, insurance, and overseas investments.

5. Branches of Commerce: Transport

1. When choosing a form of transport for a consignment of goods a businessman would bear the following points in mind:

(a) The degree of urgency.

(b) The kind of goods (fragile or perishable, etc.).

(c) The cost of the various transport methods available.

(d) The distance and position of the destination.

(e) The size of the consignment.

2. Speed and comfort.

3. Expense.

4. Railways in this country provide a comparatively *expensive* service for small consignments over short distances but a cheap form of transport for *bulky* consignments over *lengthy* journeys. The longer the journey the *cheaper* the rate per mile per ton. Such a scale of charges is known as a *tapered scale*.

Rail fares are fixed by an *independent* tribunal because British Rail have a *monopoly* of rail transport in this country. Rail fares are based on *"what the traffic will bear"*. Expensive, finished products are carried at a *higher* rate than crude, raw materials.

5. The use of the railway systems involves the goods in a good deal of handling. It would, therefore, pay a businessman to consider the advantages to fragile goods of "door-to-door" road transport or the more gentle method of canal transport.

Secondly, it will be cheaper for a consignment of moderate size over medium distances to be sent by road haulage.

6. Perishable or urgent goods are usually sent by passenger train for speed. *Examples:* flowers, mushrooms, bees, pigeons, mail, newspapers.

7. The canals fell into disrepair when the railways began to offer a faster means of transport and then "bought up" the canals to rid themselves of competition.

8. The two disadvantages of canal transport today in this country are: (a) it is a slow means of transport; (b) so many canals are closed down due to the state of disrepair into which they have fallen that one is limited to only a handful of "routes".

9. A liner sails along set routes or "lines" at regular intervals, hence the term "liner".

10. A tramp steamer is a ship which does not follow any particular route and sails at no fixed time. It goes wherever freight business is to be had.

11. A charter-party is a contract between the owners of a ship (or aircraft) and a businessman who wishes to hire the craft or part of the craft to carry freight either for a particular journey or for a specified period of time.

12. A shipping broker is an agent who negotiates shipping space on vessels on behalf of a client.

13. The Baltic Exchange, in London.

14. Coasters carry the following goods most commonly: coal, approximately four-fifths of the coasting trade being with grain, cement and petrol, other bulk cargoes being involved to a lesser degree. The coaster trade flourishes most on the east coast of Britain.

15. (a) Cheaper than air or rail transport.

(b) Door-to-door service results in minimum handling and risk of damage.

(c) Personal service.

(d) Road transport represents a reasonably fast service.

16. No.

17. No.

18. The road haulage men themselves.

19. Road haulage is a cheaper service than rail because it does not have to bear the heavy overhead expenses which the railways must incur.

20. (a) Comparative cheapness of the service.

(b) Door-to-door service results in minimum handling of goods.

(c) Road transport provides a convenient and reasonably swift method of transport.

(d) Most of the road haulage firms are small, and usually small firms will give a more personal service and be keener to give good service than will larger, more impersonal State-run enterprises.

21. No, a *great* increase in the amount of goods carried by road transport is unlikely due to the ever-increasing problem of congestion in and around our major cities.

22. Canals offer *cheap* transport.

23. Coal constitutes about half the total tonnage carried by canal, with sundry bulk items such as timber, sand, flour and pottery making up the rest.

24. The Manchester Ship Canal.

6. *Branches of Commerce: Insurance*

1. Lloyd's.

2. *Lloyd's List.*

3. Syndicates are groups of underwriters at 'Lloyd's who appoint an underwriting agent to accept insurance risks on the behalf of the whole group. Since each syndicate is made up of a large number of individual underwriters, the agent is able to accept large portions of a risk, which risk is then shared by all members of the syndicate. The 5700 underwriting members of Lloyd's have formed themselves into about 280 syndicates.

4. An insurance broker is an agent who acts on behalf of a customer who wishes to take out a policy. He is responsible for finding his client the underwriter or insurance company who offers the most satisfactory terms for his particular insurance need.

5. In fact, these two words are of identical meaning. However, the custom has developed of treating assurance as referring to life assurance and insurance as referring to all other forms of insurance.

6. In the early days of fire-insurance, insurance companies ran their own fire-brigades in an effort to keep claims down. When a householder took out an insurance policy for fire with such a company, they would fix a special plate to his wall to show their brigade that he was a policy-holder and entitled to all possible assistance in the event of a fire. This identifying plate was called a "fire-mark".

7. The three principles upon which all insurance is based are: (a) utmost good faith, (b) insurable interest, and (c) indemnity.

8. Utmost good faith means that both parties to an insurance contract, the insurer and the insured, must be completely honest with each other and not hold back any relevant facts when arranging the insurance cover. The insurer must tell the insured clearly what the terms of the insurance are and the insured must divulge all the material facts to the insurers.

An example of a material fact which would affect the policy might be, in the case of life assurance, the assured who failed to divulge all relevant information as to his health, such as a history of tuberculosis or thrombosis. Under the utmost-good-faith principle, if either of these material facts were withheld by the assured, his policy would become null and void.

9. This principle means that it is only possible to insure against events or misfortunes which cause the insured some loss of right, liability or finance. Insurable interest is limited to one's *financial interest* in the object of the insurance, although no limit is put on the value of a person's life in the case of life assurance. If it were possible to insure against events which would in no way affect one, insurance would become a gamble. In fact, before insurable interest became a necessary part of all insurance contracts, people would insure the life of the king or other well-known public figure, hoping to make a profit upon his death.

10. With the exception of life assurance, of course, the object of insurance is to place the insured after a loss or liability in the same financial position as he occupied beforehand. It is important, however, that the insured should not gain more than he actually lost. If it were possible to make a profit out of an insured loss, people might be tempted to precipitate events which would result in a loss and subsequent claim. The principle of indemnity, therefore, means that one is not allowed to take out a policy which would result in one making a *profit* when the claim was made.

11. With a whole-life policy the proposer insures his life for a certain sum of money. When he dies, his family receives this sum. In an endowment assurance policy, however, the sum assured becomes payable after a fixed number of years *or* at death, if this should occur earlier. Endowment policies are a popular form of long-term saving.

12. The holder of a "with profits" policy will pay more in premiums than an ordinary policy holder, but he will become entitled to a share of the profits earned by the insurance company. Therefore, if a man takes out an endowment policy for £3000 payable at the age of 55 or at death if this should occur sooner, he or his heirs will only receive the £3000. Should he, however, take out a "with profits" policy, he or they would receive the £3000 *plus* a share of the profits earned by the insurance company. The amount of his share cannot be forecast and naturally depends upon the size of the insurance company's profits.

13. You can obtain advice on which insurer to place your business with from an *insurance broker*. You must then complete a *proposal form* and send it, together with the necessary *premium*, to the insurers. Later the broker or agent will send you an *insurance certificate* which will serve as proof that you are insured. An insurance *policy* provides written evidence of the exact details of the contract between the insurers and the insured. If you should be unfortunate enough to have an accident, you would make a *claim* for reimbursement.

14. A trader, without insurance cover, whose premises are burnt to the ground will obviously be financially ruined. If he has an adequate fire insurance policy, however, he will claim on this and be reimbursed for his loss. This payment will enable him to rebuild and restock his shop, but the reader will realize that this process is bound to take some time. In the meantime, he cannot carry on his business and earn his living, so he will still suffer considerable financial hardship. To meet this situation, a further insurance benefit has been provided. The trader can also insure against "loss of profits" following a fire. In this case, he will not only receive the money to build and equip his shop again, but will also receive a stipulated sum to reimburse him for the profits he would have earned had the shop not been destroyed. These payments will continue until he is back in business and earning profits at his original level.

15. (a) Loss of profits following alternations of good and bad trade.

(b) Loss of profits due to a fall in the value of stock following a change in fashion.

16. It must be possible for insurance companies to estimate the risk involved before they are prepared to enter into an insurance contract. If it is not possible to measure the risks according to past or comparable experience, then the insurers have nothing on which to base their calculations and insurance cannot be effected.

17. An Act of God is classified as an event which no human foresight can prevent (e.g. earthquakes, floods and damage caused by lightning are Acts of God).

18. Yes, the comparative frequency of such acts makes it possible to calculate their probability and it is possible to insure against most of them.

19. (a) No vessel would put to sea and, therefore, no export trade would be possible without the protection of insurance.

(b) Insurance is a valuable invisible export.

(c) Banks will only discount bills of exchange for goods in transit if the goods in question are fully insured. They will then accept the insurance policy as collateral security and will discount the bill. Thanks to insurance, therefore, it is possible for exporters to obtain their payment for goods quickly and so avoid the necessity of tying down large sums of capital on export trade.

20. 1908 (5s. a week pension at 70 years). Lloyd George.

21. Sickness allowances, unemployment benefits, family allowances, maternity grants, funeral grants, pensions.

22. Premiums.

23. A policy (an agreement between insurers and insured persons).

24. A mutual insurance company, which is in effect owned by its policy-holders.

25. A sharing of risk.

26. Invest it, e.g. in shares, stocks, unit trusts, property, loans.

27. Third party insurance.

28. By a fidelity bond.

29. In insurance, the higher the *risk*, the higher the *premium*.

30. About 1700.

31. Ships against shipwreck, loss, damage, fire, etc.; cargoes (loss or damage); crews and passengers and their property; delays (for various reasons), for which shipowners may have to pay cargo-owners or passengers.

32. No, it is an Association of Underwriters.

33. The underwriters (or "syndicates" of them).

34. Insurance brokers.

35. No, almost anything can be insured at Lloyd's *except* endowment business. One can insure cars, aircraft, entertainers, property, antiques. One may insure against having twins, say, or against rain spoiling a fête or holiday.

36. *Lloyd's Register of Shipping*; Lloyd's *Daily List*. The list may be read at many public libraries and it is London's oldest newspaper.

37. The Lutine Bell is rung once for bad news and twice for good news.

38. "95 A1 at Lloyd's." (A ship's condition is classified as from 75 to 100, the latter figure representing a vessel in really first-class condition.)

39. On an "original slip"—they indicate the amount they will insure and add their initials.

40. It is not limited.

41. Lloyd's underwriters have clients throughout the world, especially in the U.S.A., and this business brings in much foreign currency; such income is a valuable contribution to our invisible exports.

42. The shareholders receive the net profits from a limited (insurance) company.

43. The policy-holders receive the net profits from a mutual insurance company.

44. A comprehensive marine policy.

45. *Uberrimae fidei* is Latin for "utmost good faith". All insurance must be taken out in utmost good faith, with no deception, fraud or misleading statements by either the insurers or the insured.

46. The United States of America.

7. Branches of Commerce: Banking

1. The banks originated from gold and silver merchants who came from Lombardy in Italy.

2. Lombard Street.

3. Commercial Banks; Post Office Savings Banks; Trustee Savings Banks; Hire-purchase Finance Houses; Merchant Banks.

4. Barclays; Lloyds; Midland; National Provincial; Westminster. They are all Commercial Banks (also called Joint-stock Banks/Clearing Banks).

5. Current account and deposit account.

6. No interest is paid on a current account.

7. The deposit account does earn interest. The interest rate is usually fixed 2 per cent *below* the Bank Rate except when the Bank Rate falls below 4 per cent.

8. Stamp duty is 2d. per cheque and this duty goes to the Exchequer, the "Nation's Purse".

9. Bearer cheques are, as their name implies, payable to either the person named on the cheque or to anyone "bearing" the cheque. Therefore, a dishonest person, finding one, could go to the bank and claim payment as the "bearer". It is a little more difficult for the criminal to obtain payment fraudulently on an order cheque, since the named payee must endorse the cheque before passing it on to a third party. A dishonest finder of an order cheque would, therefore, have to forge the endorsement without knowing what the payee's signature looks like and would run the risk of the bank spotting that the signature is a forgery. There is, therefore, less risk of an order cheque going astray and so it is usual today for people to use it in preference to a "bearer" cheque.

10. Banks offer the following services:

(a) The most important service is the cheque system which is operated in conjunction with a current account. British businessmen rely upon the cheque system as a safe, speedy and convenient means of settling debts.

(b) The bank will take care of money or valuables for their customers.

(c) People who do not need to draw on their money at the bank frequently can put their savings into a deposit account at the bank to earn interest at a rate normally 2 per cent below the current Bank Rate.

(d) Loans. The banks will loan money to approved borrowers, normally against security (called "collateral").

(e) Banks discount bills of exchange.

(f) Banks provide a further method of settling debts—the Credit Transfer System.

(g) Banks will arrange for telegraphic money transfers and for letters of credit for payments abroad.

(h) Banks will give advice on a wide range of business problems, particularly regarding investments and income tax.

(i) Banks issue travellers cheques.

(j) Banks will advise regarding wills and are prepared to act as executors.

11. A cheque which is not crossed is known as an "open" cheque.

12. (a) On the front, (b) on the back.

13. Add your initials to any minor changes and sign fully near any major alterations.

14. A cheque which is dated ahead, for payment later, is known as a post-dated cheque.

15. A cheque is an *order* to a bank to pay a certain sum from the drawer's account to a certain person or to his order.

16. No, but a printed cheque form is preferable.

17. Written on a piece of paper with a 2d. stamp added.

18. An overdraft is, with permission from the bank, the drawing out of more than is in one's bank account.

19. Security such as documents, policies, property which are worth money and which a lender may sell to raise money if his loan is not repaid.

20. Broadly speaking, banks earn money by "borrowing" from their customers (by using money left in deposit and current accounts), and then investing or lending this money at interest.

(a) Banks loan money at interest to their own customers.

(b) Banks discount bills of exchange.

(c) Banks invest money in safe securities, such as Government Stock.

(d) Banks make short-term loans to bill-brokers and members of the Stock Exchange.

(e) Banks also earn money by charging their customers for the provision of current account facilities (bank charges) and by making charges for special services or advice.

21. No, the details of your account are confidential and all bank staff are sworn to secrecy.

22. The paying-in book is the customer's record of all deposits. The bank clerk will check that the money, cheques, etc., being paid in are as described on the paying-in book and will then sign and stamp the paying-in book with the bank's official stamp.

23. The bank statement represents a complete record of all transactions within an account. It will record the money deposited in the first instance, all further payments made into the account, together with details of all payments made by cheque or cash. It will also show a running balance.

24. Cheques themselves have not passed *through* the Central Clearing House since 1939. The head offices of the clearing banks now do the sorting and distribution of cheques between themselves and only send the total amounts concerned to the Central Clearing House so that the clearing calculations can be made.

25. The clearing banks send the Central Clearing House, at the end of each day, a complete record of all cheques passed from one bank to another. It is the function of the Central Clearing House then to make the calculations necessary to determine how much money each bank owes the others. It sends its calculations to the Bank of England, where the necessary balances are transferred between banks in the process of "settling up".

26. A crossed cheque must be paid into the credit of a bank account. It cannot be exchanged for cash across the counter of a bank, and so is a safeguard against the money being paid to the wrong person. Crossing does not prevent loss or theft of cheques but does act as a deterrent to the dishonest since it makes it possible to trace a thief through the account into which he paid the cheque.

27. A standing or banker's order represents instructions to a bank to pay a specified sum of money to a named person or institution regularly on given dates in the future, and until instructed to stop these payments. Many people pay their insurance premiums, hire-purchase payments, mortgage payments, club subscriptions, motoring organization subscriptions, etc., in this way, and so this system eliminates the possibility of a customer ever forgetting to make a due payment.

28. When a person arranges a bank loan the sum of money borrowed is put to the credit of his account. The borrower then pays interest on the loan, whether or not he actually uses the money placed in his account.

When a person arranges to have an overdraft he has requested the bank to meet and pay cheques up to a specified figure more than he actually has in his account. He then pays interest only on the actual sum he overdraws and for the time his account is "in the red" (overdrawn). The overdraft is a cheaper form of borrowing for the customer whose loan requirements fluctuate or who needs to borrow for very short periods.

29. No, cash is available on demand.

30. Yes, it is usual for banks to expect from 7 to 14 days' notice of withdrawal.

31. It is a Court Order to restrain a bank from paying out a customer's money until the court instructs otherwise.

32. An order cheque which is endorsed becomes a bearer cheque to all intents and purposes. One could also change the instructions from "Pay ... or Order" to "Pay ... or Bearer", or simply write "Pay Bearer" instead of naming a special payee.

33. The nation.

34. It is the "Bankers' Bank".

35. The person to whom the cheque is made payable is the payee.

36. A crossed cheque cannot be *cashed* at a commercial bank. It can only be paid into the credit of an account, to be drawn on three days later.

37. The cheque system.

38. (i) Refer to drawer, (ii) insufficient funds, (iii) not sufficient funds.

39. A cheque then becomes negotiable.

40. The pawnbroker's sign originated from part of the crest of an Italian banking family (de Medici) who dealt in gold and silver. Their hanging sign was soon seen by people wishing to borrow money against their gold and silver goods.

41. The Bank of England was founded in 1694 and nationalized in 1946. (Note the same figures in these dates.)

42. 10s.; £1; £5; £10 (*former* higher values were withdrawn many years ago. No higher new issues are contemplated.)

43. Bank of England; Bank of Scotland; Bank of Ireland.

44. The Treasury.

45. About 10 per cent is kept as "till money".

46. It is lent, at interest, or invested. Some is also kept at the Bank of England—the "Bankers' Bank".

47. Bank charges are calculated on the number of transactions entered in a customer's account together with the average balance maintained in the account (i.e. the bank might waive charges if a customer keeps a high balance in his account, since the bank will be earning money themselves by loaning out the deposited money).

48. The Bank Rate is the rate at which first-class bills of exchange are discounted by the Bank of England. When the Bank Rate is raised borrowing becomes more expensive and so is reduced.

49. No.

50. "W. Dear, wife of John Dear."

51. "H. Dunkley; J. Dunkley" (i.e. mistaken name and correct name).

52. Joint stock banks; clearing banks.

53. Hire-purchase finance houses.

54. (a) The drawer signs his name on the front of a cheque.

(b) The payee endorses a cheque by writing his signature on the back.

55. By writing between the lines of the crossing the name of the person you wish to receive the money and adding the branch bank at which he keeps his account. One could, alternatively, write "Account payee only" between the lines of the crossing.

56. The bank will not pay the cheque before the date marked upon it.

57. Money or documents (bills of exchange, cheques etc.) which may be passed on to someone else in settlement of a debt.

58. A stale cheque is one which is presented for payment more than 6 months after the date shown on it.

59. Any cheque which is not specially crossed.

60. Yes, the X is the man's signature or sign.

61. A high Bank Rate.

8. Bills of Exchange

1. The creditor draws up the bill of exchange.

2. The debtor draws up a cheque.

3. The Bills of Exchange Act, 1882.

4. The foreign bill of exchange is the most commonly used today.

5. The need for inland bills of exchange has diminished since most suppliers are prepared to grant reasonable credit to home market customers. The inland bill of exchange has been largely replaced by a cheque or, if further credit is required, by a bank loan or overdraft.

6. A bill is known as a "draft" until it has been accepted.

7. After the bill has been accepted it is known as an "acceptance".

8. To discount a bill of exchange is to sell it to a banker, less the discount charge the bank will make for its services. (The bank is virtually loaning this sum of money for the period of time the bill has to run.)

9. A letter of hypothecation is a document which authorizes a bank to sell the goods covered by the bill of exchange in the event of the "buyer" failing to accept or pay the bill.

10. A cheque is a bill of exchange drawn on a banker and payable on demand.

11. They need not pay, or accept as the case may be, the bill of exchange until they have seen the goods arrive and checked to see that they are as ordered and in sound condition. Secondly, provided the bill is not a bill of sight, the debtor is granted a period of credit and can often sell the goods concerned before he is required to pay for them, without straining his financial resources.

12. Firstly, the exporter may be reluctant to send off valuable goods without being sure that he will be paid for them. He can, however, send a bill of exchange with the shipping documents to his bank's representatives in the country concerned, together with full instructions in writing. The foreign bank will then notify the importer, who must accept or pay the bill before the bank will hand over the necessary shipping documents for him to claim the goods from the Customs. In this way the exporter knows that the goods will not be handed over until the customer has accepted or paid the bill.

Secondly, the exporter can obtain the money due for the consignment of goods (less the discounting charge) by taking the bill of exchange to the bank to be discounted.

13. Firstly, a bill of exchange has to be accepted by the debtor and a cheque does not. Secondly, a bill is drawn up by the creditor whereas a cheque is made out by the debtor. Thirdly, a bill of exchange states the length of time the bill has to run before payment, whereas a cheque is payable on demand.

14. You can buy a blank inland bill of exchange from any Post Office.

15. Three days of grace.

16. 6 July, 1966.

17. 2d.

18. 2d.

19. When a bank discounts a bill of exchange which is subsequently dishonoured they are entitled to demand payment from the drawer of the bill (the creditor).

20. The drawee accepts a bill of exchange by writing "Accepted" and his signature across the face of the bill.

21. When the drawer wishes his debtor (the drawee) to pay the money to a third party (e.g. when A. Johnson draws up a bill not payable to himself but "Three months after date pay to J. Duggan, Lloyds Bank, Stockport the sum of fifty pounds. Value received").

22. The bill may be made payable "to me or my order".

23. A bill of exchange may be restricted by making it payable to "me only" or "payee only".

24. One could sell it or discount it, through a bank, bill broker or discount house.

25. Usually at, or very near, Bank Rate.

26. It is evidence that the acceptor admits his debt to the drawer for a certain sum and undertakes to pay this sum by a certain date.

27. To a bank or bill broker is the simplest way.

28. To overcome currency difficulties; to postpone payment of the bill until buyer and seller are satisfied about their transaction; to enable the seller to obtain his money quickly by discounting the bill.

29. A bill is dishonoured when (a) the drawee fails to accept the bill; or (b) the drawee has already accepted the bill but refused payment.

30. When an inland bill is dishonoured, a notary public (often a solicitor) may be employed to present it again for payment and then he notes on the bill the non-payment, with reasons, and the date.

31. Noting prevents any future dispute about the presentation of the bill.

9. *Communications and the Post Office*

1. Yes.

2. Letter post.

3. The address should be written clearly and contain:

(a) The name of the addressee.

(b) The number of the house (or name, if no number allocated) or flat and the name of the street or road.

(c) The name of the village or district.

(d) The name of the **POST TOWN** (in block letters) followed in the case of large cities by the district initials and/or numbers.

(e) The name of the county in which the post town is situated.

(f) The address should be written in the lower half of the envelope so that the post-mark and stamp do not obliterate any of the address.

Examples:

T. Dowman, Esq.,
28 Manor Park Rise,
Cottingham,
HULL,
East Yorkshire.

J. Tomlinson, Esq.,
4 Abercrombie Way,
LONDON, S.W.2.

4. When the need for communication is urgent.

5. One should follow up with a letter confirming the details of the conversation on the telephone.

6. One should say one's telephone number and name.

7. In a telephone directory.

8. In a classified directory.

9. Directory inquiries.

10. 22 lb.

11. *The Post Office Guide* or *Whitaker's Almanack*.

12. (a) By filling in a form and handing it over the counter at a Post Office, with the appropriate payment.

(b) By giving your message and the appropriate fee to a telegraph boy.

(c) By dictating your telegram over the telephone to the inland telegrams operator.

13. 5s. 6d.

14. 5d.

15. 8d. He pays double the value of the stamp which was not attached.

16. £10.

17. Apply to the Postmaster-General on a Post Office form and a crossed warrant will be issued to enable a larger sum to be withdrawn.

18. Money orders, postal orders, registered letters, crossed warrants, telegraphic money orders.

19. (a) Letter post.

(b) Parcel post.

(c) Letter post.

(d) Railex.

(e) A telegram, if he was staying at an address without a telephone.

Note:—The Police would also be prepared to pass on an urgent message quickly.

(f) Recorded delivery or registered post.

(g) Registered post.

(h) Telegraphic money order.

20. 6d.–£5.

21. A postal order may be crossed. It must then be paid into an account at the savings bank or a commercial bank.

22. (a) Yes, a postal order may be paid into an account at the Post Office.

(b) Yes, a postal order may also be paid into an account at a bank.

23. £50. Also called a Post Office Order (P.O.O.).

24. (a) $2\frac{1}{2}$ per cent; (b) the same, $2\frac{1}{2}$ per cent.

25. £15.

10. *Advertising and Market Research*

1. The two basic functions of advertising are: (a) to provide information; (b) to persuade people to buy.

2. A trade mark is a sign or symbol used by firms to identify their products or to help to fix their name firmly in the public eye.

3. Advertising agents.

4. Advertising agents earn commission on all advertisements they place for their clients in printing, newspapers, television, etc.

5. (a) Advertising on commercial television and radio.

(b) Advertising in newspapers and magazines.

(c) Advertising in cinemas.

(d) Counter and window displays.

(e) Posters in buses and trains.

(f) Advertising on hoardings.

(g) Samples, free gifts, competitions, cut-price coupons, etc.

6. Advertising costs account for approximately:

10 per cent of the production costs of food and general household goods.

35 per cent of the production costs of patent foods and general toilet requisites.

45 per cent of the production costs of patent medicines.

7. Advertising, by introducing consumers to the latest labour-saving devices, contributes to our rising *standard* of *living*.

8. Mail-order and direct-selling concerns rely 100 per cent on advertising in making their approach to the consumer.

9. The constant repetition of the television advertising slogan probably amounts to mass *hypnotism*.

10. High-pressure advertising encourages people to live *beyond* their *means* and to make them *discontented*.

11. Market research organizations gauge the potential market for a product and also ascertain the needs and desires of the public.

12. They ask a comparatively small number of people (a "sample") what their opinions are and from these results they "scale up" their findings to cover the whole population for potential customers.

13. The comparatively small sample of people may not be representative. The researchers must be very careful to have a true cross-section of the public or the results could be inaccurate.

14. A department store would wish to advertise extensively up to a radius of between 10 and 50 miles, depending upon the part of the country concerned, and would be likely to advertise in local newspapers, on hoardings, at local cinemas and just possibly on regional television, as well as having good window displays.

15. A breakfast cereal firm would have a nation-wide market and would want the most extensive advertising campaign possible. They would use national commercial television advertising, radio advertisements, national newspapers and magazines, together with shop displays.

16. The advantage of the branded-goods system to the customer is that he or she can always be sure that a particular brand's quality will remain consistent wherever it is purchased, or at whatever price the shopkeeper sells it for.

17. With the help of advertising, the manufacturer can ensure that everyone is familiar with his branded product and can take action, by registration, to see that no other manufacturer tries to imitate his brand or trade mark.

11. How Business Is Transacted: Documents

1. Retailers can find out about the range of goods available in their trade by attending trade exhibitions, by taking specialized trade journals, by talking to commercial travellers, and by visiting wholesale warehouses and discussing their problems with the management.

2. A catalogue is a booklet containing illustrations and a complete description of goods offered for sale.

3. A price list is, as its name implies, a list of articles and their prices. Since prices often fluctuate, many suppliers issue supplementary price lists of the items in the catalogues, so that when prices change the expensive catalogues do not have to be scrapped. New price lists would be printed and issued with the original catalogues.

4. When a retailer has decided what he will buy from a wholesaler, he will send the wholesaler an *order*. If the wholesaler has these goods in stock, he will draw up at least four basic documents. These are:

(a) An original *invoice*.
(b) A copy *invoice*.
(c) A *packing slip*.
(d) A *delivery note*.

An original invoice will be sent to the *purchaser* and the copy invoice will be kept and given to the *Accounts* Department. The packing slip is sent to the *Dispatch* Department so that they know what to pack and where to send the consignment. The delivery note is sent with the goods so that the retailer can *check* the consignment.

5. An invoice is a document setting out the quantity, general information and the prices of goods sold to the purchaser. It is this document which tells the purchaser how much he owes for a particular consignment.

6. A delivery note is the document sent, with the goods, to the customer. It enables him to check the goods against those listed on the delivery note. If satisfied that the goods are not damaged he will sign to say that the consignment has been received in good order.

7. The supplier would keep his copy of the invoice so that his accountants could keep a record of the amount owed to the business by the customer invoiced.

8. Normally, a supplier will send his customers a *statement* of *account* at the end of the month.

9. A statement of account is, in effect, a copy of the customer's account as it appears in the seller's ledger.

10. A credit note is used when goods, already invoiced, are found by the buyer to be damaged, or not as ordered. In such cases the seller will send the buyer a credit note for the value of the goods returned, to be set against (or reduce) the amount originally invoiced. Credit notes can also be used to correct inadvertent arithmetical or typewriting errors on invoices which have been sent to customers. Credit notes indicate to the customer that his account in the seller's ledger has been credited with the sum stated. This means that the sum the debtor owes has been reduced by the amount shown on the credit note.

11. Debit notes are sent to a customer to inform him that his account in the seller's ledger has been debited (charged) with the sum stated, together with the reason for this. Debit notes are not so common as credit notes and are used to adjust under-charges.

12. Trade discount is the amount allowed off the price of goods to shopkeepers and others "in the trade". It is the difference between the price the retailer pays for an article and what he charges the public and, therefore, constitutes his margin of gross profit. It is upon trade discount that the trader relies to pay his expenses and to earn his livelihood.

13. Cash discount is a deduction allowed to encourage purchasers to settle their debts promptly. The quicker they pay their accounts, usually the larger the discount.

14. A cheque is in itself a receipt since it will return to the drawer, through the Clearing House circuit, after it has been met.

15. A statement is a copy of the customer's account as it appears in the seller's ledger and will, therefore, contain the amounts owing from the various invoices sent during the month, together with details of any payments already received from the customer. It will also show the outstanding balance. An invoice, on the other hand, is confined to showing how much the customer *owes* for one particular consignment.

12. Types of Business Ownership

1. The different forms of business organization can be compared under the following headings:

  (a) How they obtain their capital.

  (b) How they control the business.

  (c) How they deal with profits or losses.

2. The sole trader himself is responsible for all the debts of his business, even to the extent of his private means.

3. The sole trader provides the capital himself, either from his own savings or by borrowing.

4. The sole trader controls the business himself.

5. If there is a profit, it goes (less income tax) to the sole trader to do with as he wishes.

6. An ordinary (or simple) partnership consists of from two to twenty persons.

7. Ordinary (or simple) partnerships are governed by the Partnership Act of 1890.

8. If no Articles of Partnership have been drawn up, then under the Partnership Act of 1890 the following conditions apply:

  (a) Profits must be divided equally and partners must contribute equally to any losses.

  (b) No partner is entitled to interest on capital.

  (c) No partner is entitled to salary for acting in the partnership business.

  (d) Loans or advances by a partner to the firm must bear interest at the rate of 5 per cent per annum.

Although they share the financial burden, each partner is, like the sole trader, responsible for debts of the business to the extent of his private means should the business fail.

97

9. Each partner is responsible for debts of the business even to the extent of his private means.

10. A limited partner is one whose liability is limited to the amount of money he has invested. Limited partners, however, must not take any part in the running of the business.

11. Sleeping or dormant partners are the inactive ones in a business.

12. No, the Limited Partnership Act of 1907 states that there must also be at least one general partner in all limited partnerships.

13. In a limited company it is the shareholders' liability that is limited to the amount of money they have invested.

14. A public company obtains its capital from shares, stocks, debentures and loans.

15. A public company is controlled by a managing director and a board of directors elected by the shareholders.

16. The net profits of public companies are distributed, at the discretion of the directors, to the shareholders in the form of dividends.

17. Private and public companies.

18. A private company may have from two to fifty shareholders, plus present or past members of the staff.

19. No.

20. Public joint stock companies sell their shares on the Stock Exchange.

21. Private limited companies sell shares to members of the family, friends, acquaintances, staff, etc. A shareholder is not allowed to transfer his shares without the consent of his fellow shareholders.

22. The capital of co-operative societies is mainly provided by its member/customers. Each member pays an entrance fee of 1s. and is required to take out a £1 share in the society.

23. The members of the co-operative societies elect a president and committee to appoint staff and administer the business for them.

24. The net profits are distributed among members, in proportion to their purchases, in the form of dividends.

25. Local government enterprises obtain capital from local rates, by issuing stocks and by grants and loans from the Government.

26. Services run by local authorities are administered by committees appointed by the local council.

27. Any net profits made by local government undertakings either result in lower charges for the service concerned, or go to swell the coffers of the local authority and so, in theory, subsidize the ratepayer.

28. Nationalized enterprises are financed by the Government from taxation and, of course, by making charges for the services provided, and by issue of gilt-edged stock.

29. Public corporations organized by members who are appointed by the relevant Minister (Railways—Minister of Transport). The Minister is responsible for the overall running of the service, but does not concern himself with its day-to-day working. The individual consumer's interests are safeguarded by consumer councils and by Members of Parliament. The Minister can be questioned by Members of Parliament on important matters concerning the service.

30. Any net profits made by State-owned enterprises go to provide cheaper services or are used to alleviate taxation.

31. *Examples:*
(a) In the case of such services as electricity, water, gas and telephones, it would be inconvenient and wasteful to permit a number of organizations to dig up roads on many occasions simply to duplicate services. It is best that each service be streamlined and placed in the hands of one Board.
(b) Goods and materials can be bought in bulk and therefore at lower prices.
(c) Essential industries should be nationalized so that they can be run for the benefit of the nation, rather than for the financial benefit of shareholders.

   (d) To avoid exploitation of the public by a monopoly, in the case of essential services (coal, electricity, gas and transport). Some argue that if there is monopoly, it is best that the Government should control it for the benefit of the general public.

   (e) Under State control, the area electricity boards are connected by the grid system and, in the event of generator breakdown in one area, the other boards supply current until repairs are carried out. This arrangement makes for greater efficiency and ensures a more reliable, regular supply of electricity to the consumer.

   (f) Government funds can be used to modernize and provide research for industry. Joint stock companies would not have the financial resources to do so and would be distracted by the profit motive.

   (g) The Government safeguards the interests of workers.

   (h) Profits are not paid out to shareholders, but go to benefit the public in the form of lower charges for services concerned or by lessening taxation.

32. *Examples:*

   (a) The rigid pattern of bureaucratic administration kills the initiative of workers within the industry.

   (b) The success or failure of the business is not so personal to the men in control, since they have not invested money in it.

   (c) Lack of competition results in a falling off of efficiency (the spur of competition keeps many businessmen on their toes).

Also, in the event of any trading losses, the Government will always subsidize the industry out of taxes. A nationalized industry run inefficiently, as a result of the above points, can whittle away government funds and become a heavy burden upon the taxpayer.

33. The shareholders' financial liability is limited to paying the full amount they have been asked to pay for their shares.

34. It is "incorporated".

35. Private and public.

36. The Companies Act, 1948, which consolidated (joined together) many earlier Acts.

37. The Registrar of Joint Stock Companies (City Road, London E.C.1).

38. The Memorandum of Association; Articles of Association.

39. In the Memorandum, at least:

(a) The name of the company, plus "limited".

(b) Where the registered office of the company will be.

(c) The objects for which the company is formed.

(d) That the liability of members is limited.

(e) The maximum capital to be raised, and in what form (debentures, preference shares, ordinary shares, etc.).

40. The Articles of Association contain the rules drawn up for running the company (e.g. about chairman for meetings, number of votes for each shareholder, payment to directors).

41. From two to twenty; except in a bank, which may have from two to ten partners.

42. Fifty (plus present or past staff).

43. There must be at least seven, but there is no upper limit for the number of shareholders (but the amount of permitted capital does limit the number).

44. At least a (company) secretary and one director.

45. He would then have limited liability and in the event of failure would not have to sell up everything he owned.

He would also be able to raise a great deal more capital through the other shareholders.

46. Auditing means the examining/checking of the accounts by a duly authorized person (usually a qualified accountant), and verifying by reference to vouchers, receipts, cheque books, etc.

47. A public limited company must send each year a copy of the audited profit and loss account and balance sheet to the Registrar of Joint Stock Companies.

48. They must be audited.

49. At the office of the Registrar of Joint Stock Companies.

50. The records are available to public inspection to enable traders, investors or other interested parties to read the company's registered documents, including the annual accounts; this is a safeguard to such people.

51. In its Memorandum of Association.

52. A board of directors (with one usually as managing director).

53. An overdraft; a short-term loan; (sometimes) a long-term loan.

54. Collateral. Some document representing property (e.g. a house) or the property itself (e.g. jewellery, valuable painting).

55. The internal rules for running the company (concerning directors, shareholders' voting rights, etc.).

56. Public, because public limited companies can usually have more shareholders than are permitted for private limited companies.

57. No.

58. Entrepreneur.

59. Sole trader.

60. The contributing retail co-operative societies.

61. Electricity; gas; transport; water.

62. The nationalized utilities are electricity and gas. Transport is partly nationalized (e.g. British Rail and British Road Services, but the remainder of road transport is run by private enterprise).

63. Most nationalization has occurred since 1946.

64. Government stock.

65. Some local authorities (councils); mostly water boards.

66. (a) There is a linked-up country-wide supply (national grid) to help out, especially when breakdowns occur locally; (b) charges and prices are fairly level everywhere. (In London alone the charges some years ago used to vary from borough to borough from one-eighth of a penny to about 1s. 6d. a unit!)

67. British Rail.

68. A Minister (e.g. Minister of Transport, Minister of Power).

69. An Area Board.

70. By the sale of government stock, e.g. electricity, 5 per cent 1975.

71. They are nearly all monopolies. If we want gas, electricity or water we have no choice of suppliers.

72. *Examples:* Board of Trade, the Treasury, Ministry of Transport, Ministry of Agriculture and Fisheries, Department of Education and Science, Ministry of Power, Ministry of Labour, Ministry of Health (although probably *all* departments are concerned in some way with Commerce).

73. The Bank of England (nationalized in 1946).

74. The President (of the Board of Trade).

75. Home trade; foreign trade.

13. Stock Exchanges/Stocks/Shares

1. A stock exchange is a market for securities.

2. Members of the public are not permitted to buy and sell securities in person because it would be quite impossible for all who wish to buy and sell shares to trade in a stock exchange at once. Further, nobody would know anyone else and it would be easy for unscrupulous men to swindle inexperienced members of the public.

3. There are twenty-three stock exchanges in Britain; the main one is in London.

4. A stockbroker acts as agent for investors who wish to buy or sell securities.

5. A jobber is a specialist in buying and selling securities relating to a particular industry. A jobber deals only with stockbrokers.

6. Securities.

7. Gilt-edged securities are government or local authority stocks (fixed term loans) and represent very sound investments, since the risk is so small, hence the term "gilt-edged".

8. A debenture is a very safe form of investment. Debentures represent loans to a company as opposed to shares in it. The holders do not, therefore, have any say in the running of the company or the election of directors. Debentures are a particularly safe form of investment because debenture-holders, as creditors, are entitled to interest on their loans before any profits are distributed. In fact, if for any reason the company failed to make these payments, debenture-holders would be entitled to sell up the business in order to obtain their due interest and loan repayments. Debentures are often thought of as being similar to a mortgage, and are one of the safest securities available.

9. Interest.

10. The debentures are backed by the assets of the company.

11. Debenture-holders have no voting rights.

12. If business is good and a large profit has been made, the directors may recommend that holders of ordinary shares receive substantial dividends.

13. If business is poor, ordinary shareholders may receive little or no dividend at all.

14. Ordinary shareholders are entitled to attend the annual general meeting of their company and to vote at the election of directors.

15. Preference shareholders receive preference in the sense that they receive their dividends from the profits *before* the ordinary shareholders receive theirs from what remains.

16. Debenture-holders have first call on the profits of a company.

17. The holder of cumulative preference shares receives arrears of dividends not paid in lean years when higher profits are made in fat years.

18. An "A" ordinary share has no voting rights.

19. The "par value" of a share is its face or nominal value, i.e. what it is called (1s. share, 10s. share, etc.), and *not* the market value.

20. No: *examples:* 1s., 3s., 10s., 15s., 20s.

21. Dividend.

22. A broker (a bank or solicitor would be prepared to buy them from a broker on behalf of clients).

23. Not usually, but a company may pay a dividend from reserves or holders of cumulative preference shares *may* receive this year's unpaid dividend in the next year if profits permit.

24. No.

25. In the Memorandum of Association.

26. (a) The Bank of England; (b) the taxpayers.

27. A share warrant is an order (very like a cheque) from a limited company to a bank to pay a certain sum to a certain person in respect of dividends on shares.

28. *Examples:* shares; stocks; debentures.

29. The Stock Exchange Council runs the London Stock Exchange.

30. You may see lists of latest share prices in the daily and evening newspapers (also, more detailed, in the daily *Financial Times*).

31. About 13,000.

32. A stockbroker.

33. Jobbers.

34. The jobber's "bit" or "turn".

35. A contract note.

36. A share certificate.

37. In the Register of Shareholders.

38. Gilt-edged stock (also applied to local government stock and some Commonwealth stocks).

39. No, foreign stock is not gilt-edged. Yes, the stock exchanges do deal in foreign shares and stocks.

40. The Bourse, in Paris.

41. New York; Wall Street.

42. £1.

43. No.

44. The Memorandum of Association.

45. The prices of shares are affected by: (a) the profits and the dividend record of the company; (b) supply and demand.

46. The interest on a preference share is fixed; an ordinary share dividend is not fixed—it may be nil, little, average or large, according to the profits for the year.

47. Deferred share. The total ordinary (or deferred) shares together are called the "Equity" of the company.

48. Cumulative preference shares.

49. Ordinary shares are more risky than preference shares because there is no fixed dividend on ordinary shares, whereas preference shareholders have a fixed interest rate and have prior call on the profits, after debenture-holders.

50. A public limited company is owned by the shareholders.

51. Yes.

52. Yes.

53. (a) Yes; (b) no, not when first issued.

54. From the secretary of the Stock Exchange or from a bank or solicitor.

55. "My Word is my Bond."

56. No.

57. Co-operative members; they can invest up to £1000 and receive interest.

58. The middle price is halfway between buying and selling price. Newspapers usually quote the middle prices.

59. The yield on shares is the return on each £100 invested in the shares.

60. *Examples:* shipping (fewer goods carried, therefore, less income), and most shares of companies concerned with commodities wanted for import or export.

61. No, not individually; the Stock Exchange Council advertises the Stock Exchange.

62. No.

63. About £100 worth (lower amounts bring him too little commission, for his expenses are high).

64. In £100 lots.

65. Yes—and it is usually given a date when the Government will buy it back (e.g. electricity 6 per cent, 1984).

66. *Examples:* insurance companies; banks; unit trusts; pension funds; investment trusts; trade unions.

67. Jobbers specialize in certain groups of shares, e.g. textiles, motor industry, insurance, aviation, gold-mines, engineering, whereas stockbrokers handle all business.

68. About £1.

69. The interest to debenture-holders.

70. Once he has paid the full price asked for the shares, the shareholder cannot be made to pay any more to the company or its creditors; his liability is limited in this way—thus, "limited" company.

71. Partly paid share or not fully paid share.

72. A speculator at the stock exchange who buys securities hoping to sell them again at a higher price is known as a "bull".

73. A speculator on the stock exchange who sells his securities because he believes prices are about to fall, with the intention of buying them back more cheaply, is a "bear".

74. A "stag" is a speculator at the stock exchange who buys up new issues with the intention of selling them quickly at a profit.

14. Capital and Profits

1. Capital can be defined as "saved-up wealth employed to produce further wealth".

2. Net profit for the year, £1600 (the difference in capital reflects the profit or loss for the year).

3. There was no profit at all. In fact, the business suffered a loss of £300.

4. That part of a firm's capital which is used to cover the running of the business and which changes its form constantly in the course of business.

5. Stock, debtors, cash in hand, and cash at bank.

6. Fixed capital is made up of that part of a firm's capital which does not change its form regularly because the items have been bought for more or less permanent use.

7. *Examples:* premises, machinery, fixtures and fittings, motor vehicles (if used in the business).

8. Working capital is the amount of money readily available or assets readily realizable in the business, e.g. stocks, debtors, short-term loans and cash. It is calculated by deducting the current liabilities from current assets.

9. If a trader wishes to calculate his profit or loss, he simply compares his *income* and *expenditure* in a certain way. He uses a *Profit and Loss* Account to find the profit or loss based on buying and selling alone. This profit is called his *gross* profit. He uses a *Trading* Account to establish the final profit after the deduction of all running or *overhead* expenses. This final profit is known as his *net* profit.

10. Stock is valued at cost price by stocktaking.

11. Stock may be shown in the Trading Account at less than its cost price only when its current retail value has fallen below its original cost from the wholesalers.

12. Never.

13. The word turnover means total net sales (sales minus any sales returns).

14. The rate of turnover calculation refers to the speed at which stock is sold in a given period of time.

15. Rate of turnover $= \dfrac{\text{sales (at cost price)}}{\text{average stock held}}$.

16. One would calculate the average stock figures by totalling the monthly stock values and dividing by twelve.

17. He could reduce his prices, offer better service or increase his market by opening new shops.

18. To produce further wealth.

19. If income is a *flow* of wealth, we might describe capital as a *stock* of wealth.

20. Plenty of natural resources (raw materials) and the optimum (right-sized) population.

21. Our standard of living will fall if fewer capital goods are produced.

22. Capital is often called "*stored up* labour".

23. The stock exchanges.

24. Depreciation Account.

15. Saving and Borrowing Money

1. By saving regularly one can accumulate money with which to buy predetermined items such as clothing, holidays, scooters, cars, or to put down a deposit on a house.

2. Budgeting is the only way to keep on an even keel in these days when advertising and hire purchase tempt us to buy more than we can comfortably afford, otherwise money seems to vanish very quickly. Rent, fares, food and other essentials must be accounted for first. If there is not any money available to meet these expenses, due to foolish expenditure on non-essentials, life can become very difficult indeed. A simple budget account enables one to avoid these financial headaches and it is best to plan the budget ahead, allowing for essentials first and only using what money remains for amusements, clothes, holidays, etc.

3. £1.

4. (a) $2\frac{1}{2}$ per cent; (b) 2 per cent below the Bank Rate, provided the Bank Rate is 4 per cent or more; (c) $2\frac{1}{2}$ per cent or more according to the type of account.

5. Building societies exist to loan money to people wishing to buy houses.

6. They raise their capital by borrowing, at interest, from the general public.

7. They use their capital to loan money to house-purchasers, at interest.

8. When the building societies loan money to house-purchasers they require security for the loan. Usually, such security is the property itself. When a loan is advanced against the security of the premises themselves, it is called a mortgage.

9. (a) 3½ per cent; (b) 3¾ per cent; but these rates vary from time to time. Income tax is paid additionally by the society.

10. 3¼ per cent, but it varies from time to time.

11. When leaving savings in the Post Office, building societies, deposit account, etc., the interest received only just makes up for the fall in the value of money over the years. By investing in a Unit Trust, however, one finds that as inflation occurs the companies raise prices and so profits should remain in line with the current value of money. Therefore, the return on the units will normally keep up with inflation. A great deal of the risk of investing is taken out by a Unit Trust's policy of spreading its investments over a number of companies, so that if some have a poor year's trading the Unit Trust investors benefit from the other firms who have obtained satisfactory profits.

12. Unit Trusts are in business to use their subscribed capital to buy shares in other companies. The income of the Trust, in the form of dividends received from its investments, is then shared out among the Trust's unit-holders in the usual way. A management company organizes this and so makes it possible for the small investor to spread his limited funds throughout a number of companies.

13. An insurance broker.

14. Premium Bonds do not carry any interest; instead they carry a chance of winning a tax-free cash prize.

15. The Post Office Savings Bank.

16. Unit Trusts.

17. In a hire-purchase transaction, the purchaser does, in fact, only *hire* the goods in question, with an *option* to buy them at the end of the hire period.

18. Therefore, the goods do *not* belong to the purchaser until the *last* instalment has been paid.

19. If the goods cost less than £2000, and more than one-third of this has been paid, the owners cannot take the goods from the purchaser without first obtaining a court order. The figure of £2000 is most important. If the total cost of the goods plus interest is £2000 or less, the consumer enjoys certain protections under the Hire Purchase Acts.

Note, too, these safeguards:

(a) Before the agreement is signed the seller must state in writing the *cash* price of the goods and the total hire-purchase price.

(b) The agreement must state the cash price and the total hire-purchase price (cash price *plus* credit charge).

(c) The agreement must contain a summary of the rights and liabilities under the Hire Purchase Acts of both the seller and the consumer. The print on the agreement must be of a reasonable size (previously the print has sometimes been so small that the customer has not read it).

(d) A copy of the agreement must be sent to the consumer within 7 days of being signed in the shop.

(e) If the agreement is signed at home ("on the doorstep") the customer has 3 days then in which to cancel the agreement if he no longer wants to have the goods.

(f) If the consumer loses track of the instalments paid, for 1s. the shop must send a record of the amounts paid and due, with all the dates.

(g) If one-third of the total cost of the goods has been paid and the consumer falls into arrears with repayments, the shop or the finance company cannot take the goods away without first obtaining a court order.

(h) The consumer can at any time return goods obtained on hire purchase. If he has paid half of the total cost the finance company cannot make him pay any more. On the other hand, if he has not paid half, he can be made to pay the balance up to half the total cost.

20. The essential difference between hire purchase and credit sales is that under hire purchase the goods do not become the property of the purchaser until he has paid the final instalment whereas, under credit sales, the goods become the property of the purchaser immediately.

21. When borrowing money from a bank, the buyer would become the owner of the car immediately. Secondly, the interest charges made by banks are lower than those of hire-purchase companies.

22. Many people feel that it is better to buy a house than to rent accommodation. They prefer to live in a house which will ultimately belong to them.

A person renting accommodation often pays out so much rent over the years that he could have bought a house for the same outlay. After years of renting, the property still does not belong to him and he must continue to pay even more rent. Had he borrowed the necessary money with which to buy a house, the property would have been his when the mortgage was paid off.

The person who buys his own home finishes up with a valuable asset, whereas the man who rents accommodation finishes up with nothing to show for his expenditure.

23. A "with profits" insurance policy is one which costs more than an ordinary insurance policy because, at maturity, it entitles the holder to a share in the company's profits. The amount of his share naturally depends upon the size of the insurance company's profits.

24. Monthly account and budget account.

25. With a monthly account one chooses goods from the store and the cost of these items is entered into the customer's account. The store then sends the customer a statement of account at the end of each month. This means, in effect, that the customer is given a month in which to pay for the goods. There is no interest charge on such an account.

The budget account, however, is available for those who cannot afford to pay cash. In this case, the borrower pays a sum of money into her budget account and is then permitted to purchase goods up to, in many stores, eight times the value of her deposit. Then she pays off the balance by instalments and could, on completion, begin the process all over again. A small interest charge is normally made on budget accounts.

26. Building societies, insurance companies and local authorities. (Some employers will also advance money to their employees to enable them to buy houses. The employees then repay the loan from their salaries.)

27. A mortgage broker.

28. Local authorities do not pay brokers commission fo ntroducing business; therefore, many brokers would be tempted to ignore local authority mortgage facilities when considering which source would best suit your needs.

16. *The Discriminating Consumer*

1. It pays to buy branded goods because one can be certain that the quality of the goods will remain constant, wherever or whenever they are purchased.

2. No. The service may prove to be worth much more than £25.

3. *Examples:*

The British Standards Institute.

The Consumers' Association—publishers of *Which?*

The Retail Trades Standards Association.

The Consumer Council—Government sponsored.

The Council of Industrial Design.

Local Authority Citizens' Advice Bureaux.

4. The British Standards Institute (B.S.I.) employs the famous "kite mark".

5. *Which?*

6. *Examples:* scouring powders, washing powders, electric kettles, drip-dry shirts, motor-cars, electric blankets, television sets, beauty aids, deodorants, life-jackets, trading stamps, slide rules, heating costs, children's tricycles, toys, model racing-car tracks, hire purchase, baby alarms, Unit Trusts, annuities.

7. Switch operators advertise in newspapers and magazines, offering new or reconditioned machinery at bargain prices (washing-machines, sewing-machines and vacuum cleaners are popular switch lines). This is not mail-order selling. In fact, the reader is not asked to send any deposit for the goods advertised. The advertiser has no intention of selling the article itself. The idea is simply to discover, as a result of the advertisement, who is thinking of buying a machine. A salesman is then sent round to the prospective purchaser. Sometimes, as in the case of a vacuum cleaner, he might bring the advertised machine, either an old one, a badly reconditioned one or a new one modified so that it works inefficiently. He will also take the opportunity to demonstrate a much more efficient, *expensive* model, which cleans satisfactorily. Sometimes the demonstrator does not even bother to bring the advertised machine, claiming that they are all sold. He then proceeds to use high-pressure salesmanship to persuade the consumer to buy the expensive model, which she could have bought at any local shop at the same price and been assured of a good after-sales service.

8. Trading stamps are simply a sales-promotion device which must be paid for by the shopkeeper. It is inevitable that the cost of these stamps will be passed on to the customer in the form of higher prices.

9. The trading stamp organizations argue that their stamps increase a trader's sales and so bring him larger profits, which will cover the cost of the stamps. Although this may be true initially, other traders, losing their customers as a result, will be forced to enter into competition and buy stamps too. Eventually, the point of local saturation will be reached when most shops will be offering trading stamps of one brand or another. When this happens, no trader will enjoy an advantage over his competitors. At this point, the cost will have to be passed on to the consumer.

10. *Caveat emptor* means "let the buyer beware" (it is up to the buyer to safeguard his own interests).

11. The *caveat emptor* ruling suffers from the disadvantage that it assumes that the buyer, not to be at any disadvantage, knows as much about the product as the seller. This is clearly a false assumption when related to the wide range of technically complicated goods retailed. The purchaser is often compelled to rely on the professional advice of the retailer (largely due to this fact, the law has been changed in a number of respects during the past century).

12. Under the Sale of Goods Act, 1893, goods must be fit for the purpose for which they are sold. If they are not, then the buyer has right of redress from the retailer. Of course, it follows that he has no such rights if he used the articles for a purpose other than that for which they were sold.

If the goods are not fit for the purpose for which they were sold, the consumer is entitled to return them to the retailer concerned and claim a refund.

If goods are sold by description, they must be as described. If the information is wrong in any way and the article has been falsely described, then the buyer can claim against the seller.

In cases of negligence, the seller can be held liable for any physical injury or damage caused by defects in the articles sold, if it can be shown that he knew of the defect, or should have known of the defect. It is most important that the defective goods be returned immediately to the retailer, otherwise one is deemed to have "accepted" them, in which case no redress can be had.

The buyer, in many cases, can charge the manufacturer of the goods with negligence if it can be shown that he should have foreseen the defect and guarded against it. The consumer can sue the manufacturer and/or the retailer for injury or damage resulting from negligence.

13. In some cases the law protects the consumer in two ways: in *civil* law as a private individual and under *criminal* law as a member of the public.

14. Rights under the Sale of Goods Act.

15. (a) By approaching the retailer or manufacturer himself.

(b) The town hall will put consumers in touch with the local Citizens' Advice Bureau, who will advise on the steps required to obtain redress.

(c) Most towns today have Chambers of Commerce, run by local tradespeople and dedicated to improving standards of retailing. Such organizations are always interested to hear genuine complaints from consumers concerning poor services and are often able to help the shopper.

118

(d) Consumers may also obtain, under the Legal Advice Scheme, half an hour's advice from a member-solicitor for only £1.

16. £1.

17. It is the consumer's duty to the community to complain to the retailer and manufacturer if dissatisfied with any product. So many manufacturers, confronted with criticism concerning their products, turn round and say, "Our goods cannot be as poor as you claim because we receive so few complaints from customers." Therefore, if you are genuinely dissatisfied with an article, tell the retailer and write and let the manufacturer know.

18. (a) The Board of Trade, but the Standards Department is now being transferred to the Department of Technology; (b) to keep standard weights and measures as a guide and protection for the whole nation, suppliers and consumers, designers and engineers, scientists and architects, so that all measurements can be based on these common "standards".

19. Parliament—through Acts and Regulations, the Board of Trade and the Department of Technology.

20. Set in the north wall of Trafalgar Square, below the National Gallery.

21. 10 lb.

22. The County Councils/County Borough Councils.

23. The local councils; Urban District Councils, Rural District Councils and Borough Councils (including County Borough Councils).

24. *Examples:* drainage; slaughter-houses; dairies; food (especially milk and meat); cafés and restaurants.

25. To a public analyst (some large councils employ their own analyst).

26. Ministry of Labour/the Home Office.

27. *Examples:* sanitation; hygiene; machines (for safety); working hours and conditions (especially for women and young people); supply of light and air; temperature.

28. Public health inspectors.

29. Yes. Such action is against the law; the offender is liable to punishment.

30. A judicial body. It is a court of law.

31. The British Standards Institution. Other associations help, too, such as the Consumers' Association, Good House-keeping Institute.

32. The Consumers' Association—publishes *Which?*

33. Competition.

34. Hire purchase; credit sales.

35. Finance houses.

36. Directly the goods are handed to the buyer (but he still has to pay for them!).

37. Claim the balance of the purchase price not yet paid.

38. Yes.

39. When all the hire-purchase instalments have been paid.

40. He must obtain an order from a court (but the court will not always give such an order).

41. (a) The cash price; (b) the total hire-purchase price—cash price plus credit charge; (c) he must send a written note with these details not more than 7 days after the goods have been hired by the customer.

42. £2000.

43. Read and understand the conditions.

44. The bank loan. Bank Rate rarely rises above 8 per cent per annum, but on some hire-purchase goods purchased through a finance house the true rate of interest often works out at 25 per cent or even more!

45. Approximately £1,000,000,000 a year is spent on goods obtained by hire purchase (approaching £20 for each of our 53,000,000 population).

46. Yes, then the business owners can use most of their money for other purposes ("put the money to work"), while over a period the machine "pays for itself".

47. The Board of Trade and to some extent the Treasury.

48. From the local Citizens' Advice Bureau. The Bureau then refers to a Central Registry which has all the details.

49. A satisfactory standard for all merchandise offered for sale.

50. The quality of the food, drugs, etc.; the local councils' officers obtain regular samples of such items from all shops, public-houses and other premises in their districts, and have the samples analysed for purity and correct contents. Suppliers and sellers may be punished severely for selling adulterated or wrongly described items.

17. Abbreviations

1. Ante meridiem (before noon).

2. Brought down (referring to money balances).

3. Bill of Exchange.

4. Bill of Lading.

5. Bills Payable.

6. Bills Receivable.

7. Carried down (referring to money balances).

8. Cost, Insurance and Freight.

9. Free on Board.

10. Quotation term meaning that the buyer must pay for goods' transport from the factory.

11. Free on Rail.

12. Errors and Omissions Excepted.

13. For example.

14. And so on.

15. I owe you. (Acknowledgement of debt. *Not* a promise to pay it, however. Therefore quite worthless.)

16. Limited.

17. Post meridiem (afternoon).

18. Promissory Note.

19. As a matter of form.

20. Steamship.

21. Refer to Drawer.

22. Credit Note.

23. Debit Note.

24. Account.

25. Cash on Delivery.

26. Free alongside.

27. Ultimo (used less frequently nowadays). Last month.
28. Instant (used less frequently nowadays). This month.
29. On Her Majesty's Service.
30. Referring to.
31. Balance Sheet.
32. Cost and Freight.
33. Deposit Account.
34. Export Credits Guarantee Department.
35. Letter of Credit.
36. Letter of Hypothecation.
37. Way Bill.

18. Sales Representatives, Agents and Markets

1. He represents several wholesalers or manufacturers, of his own choice. He is not an employee of any one firm; he is paid by commission on sales.

2. The principal.

3. A factor is an agent who has the goods to sell from his own premises and in his own name but does not own the goods.

4. A factor has the actual goods to sell but a broker usually sells or buys by lists, catalogues and samples only of the goods, which are stored elsewhere for delivery later. A broker must indicate that he is acting for someone else.

5. *Examples:* stock broker; insurance broker; tea broker; coffee broker; wool broker; cotton broker.

6. A house agent; a motor factor; a fruit factor; a coal factor.

7. To the highest bidder, provided that such bid is at or above the minimum (reserve) price which the owner has said he will accept.

8. *Examples:* antiques; paintings; furs; property; jewels; cattle; rare musical instruments and other collectors' items.

9. The best known are Sothebys and Christies, who were both founded nearly 200 years ago.

10. A *del credere* agent.

11. He finds suitable, reliable customers and he guarantees payment to the exporter; he therefore charges an extra commission (*del credere* commission) on the sales.

12. The Stock Exchange; government stock is called "gilt-edged" stock.

13. *Examples:* wool, meat, fruit (especially apples), dairy products (especially cheese, butter).

14. (a) All fish brought up the Thames, by boat, is sold by Dutch auction—the price starts high and, as it is brought down in stages by the auctioneer, the buyers interrupt (bid) at the price they are willing to pay. The fish go to the first bidder. (b) Other fish, brought in by road and rail, is sold by private treaty between the factors or wholesalers and buyers.

15. Ministry of Agriculture, Fisheries and Food.

16. The Herring Industry Board in Edinburgh, Scotland.

17. The Cabinet; and the member is the Minister of Agriculture, Fisheries and Food.

18. About 19,000,000 cwt, which is approximately 37 lb per head of population.

19. England and Wales—two-thirds; Scotland—one-third.

20. About 20,000 men.

21. Refrigeration: after 1870; canning: about 100 years ago.

22. Factors (agents) and auctioneers—both sell on a commission basis.

23. So rarely caught that it is offered to the Queen.

24. Caviar(e); pickled sturgeon-roe.

25. Japan.

26. All supplies and prices are known to the buyer; he has "perfect" knowledge of the whole market.

27. Knowledge of supplies and prices throughout the market is imperfect; the buyer may therefore pay dearly or buy only second-best commodities.

28. A monopoly—where the supplier "corners the market" (produces or buys up all available supplies) so that, with no competition, he can charge high prices by restricting the amount of goods reaching the market.

29. The Monopolies and Restrictive Practices Commission (usually called The Monopolies Commission).

30. Mainly transport, but including specialization, industrial development, communications (wireless, advertising, worldwide postal system, telephone, cables).

31. The money market.

32. The Stock Exchange.

33. Billingsgate; Smithfield; Covent Garden and Spitalfields (but there are other, smaller wholesale markets).

34. Brokers and auctioneers.

35. Near-perfect.

36. An exchange (e.g. Corn Exchange). Is there an exchange near your home?

37. Hatton Garden.

19. General Knowledge: Transport and Inventions

1. (a) About 1760; (b) the Industrial Revolution.

2. 1825; Stockton/Darlington line in Durham. George Stephenson's locomotive pulled 38 open carriages of goods and passengers at 12 miles per hour.

3. About 1850.

4. 1870; to bring beef-fat from South America to Europe to convert into the newly invented margarine.

5. 1890–1900.

6. 1903 in Carolina, U.S.A. by Orville and Wilbur Wright, for a distance of 852 feet.

7. Helicopters; auto-giros; hovercraft (in some ways).

8. Shorthand and Braille.

9. (a) Stethoscope; cardiograph machine; (b) x-rays; and, more recently, tiny cameras on the end of tubes.

10. Inventions save people time and labour.

11. Transport.

12. *Examples:* tractors, lorries, ploughs, grain harvesters, other harvesters, shearers, incubators, mechanical tools.

13. *Examples:* typewriters; shorthand; teleprinter; "inter-comm." sets; automatic letter-openers and stampers; carbon paper; "window" envelopes; cables and telegraph systems; ticker-tape; duplicators.

14. *Examples:* Terylene, Acrilan, nylon, rayon and plastics.

15. (a) Fast-moving water such as rivers and waterfalls; (b) Scotland and Wales.

16. Petroleum, diesel oil, electricity, steam (for tractors). Experiments are being carried out with atomic power.

17. Rotation of crops.

18. Specialization.

19. By patents, through the Patents Office, Board of Trade.

20. Radar (or radiolocation), by using radio beams to detect obstacles in darkness and fog.

21. *Examples:* refrigeration; canning; gas preserving; air-tight bottles; vacuum containers.

22. Pasteurization (sterilization of milk by high temperatures); by Louis Pasteur, a Frenchman.

23. The internal-combustion engine.

24. Marconi in 1896. In 1902 he sent his first trans-Atlantic messages.

25. Made public in 1925/6 by John Logie Baird.

26. Amongst other things, the telephone; *c.* 1876 in America.

27. Ultimately it is the Ministry of Transport; more directly the various Boards for each transport service, e.g. British Rail, London Transport Board.

28. During the early stages of the Industrial Revolution, from approximately 1760 to 1830; they were replaced to a great extent by the railways.

29. *Examples:* petroleum; diesel oil; milk; grain; concentrated natural gas.

30. Pipes.

31. Water; gas; powdered coal in water; petroleum; cables for electricity.

32. 1869, in France by Mouries. It was developed then by two Dutch families who are still famous producers of margarine.

33. From the Greek word "margarites" meaning pearls.

34. Sir Alexander Fleming, in 1928.

35. This is impossible to say; some cumbersome models were made over 150 years ago. Typewriters have been in use for the best part of a century but on a large scale for only about 50 years.

36. In 1944. Invented by Whinfield and Dickson. Not produced in large quantities until 1954.

20. General Knowledge: Food Production and Distribution

1. About 50 per cent; the remainder is imported.

2. *Examples:* palm (kernels); ground-nuts (pea-nuts); soya beans.

3. Maize; in the corn belt of the U.S.A.

4. Refrigeration.

5. Sugar-beet.

6. Subsidies (e.g. for milk, cereals, eggs, fatstock).

7. Hops, in Kent mostly.

8. *Examples:* bottling; canning; drying; smoking; de-hydrating; keeping in gas chambers; covering well (e.g. potatoes in earth clamps).

9. In order, most is spent on meat/meat preparations; fruit and vegetables; cereals; coffee, tea and cocoa; dairy products, eggs and honey.

10. The local councils; Urban District, Borough and Rural District Councils.

11. A Public Analyst.

12. Not for human consumption, but for animals' winter feed.

13. The price will almost certainly rise.

14. The prices will tend to rise because the supply of such substitutes is limited and there will be a greater demand for them.

15. The County Councils (and the County Borough Councils).

16. Ghana.

17. In order of cost: meat (frozen, chilled or canned); sugar and syrups; butter; fruits (fresh and preserved); wheat; raisins; eggs.

18. The United Kingdom.

19. Covent Garden/Spitalfields (fruit and vegetables); Smith-field (meat and poultry); Billingsgate (fish/shellfish); others are Leadenhall (meat and poultry); London Fruit Exchange; Borough Market (fruit and vegetables).

20. *Examples:* Milk Marketing Board, Egg Marketing Board, Potato Marketing Board.

21. A lion.

22. About 300,000.

23. (a) Cider; (b) whisky; (c) beer, especially "Burton" ale; (d) whisky and Guinness stout.

24. Sheet steel, lined thinly with tin as a safeguard against infecting the contents of the can.

25. Kippers and bloaters.

26. To the Roman Catholic countries in particular. They have meatless days.

27. Argentina.

28. Yeast.

29. 8 lb (not the usual 14 lb).

30. The haddock; you can see the marks on the haddock's "neck" (this is the fish reputed to have been used in the "feeding of the five thousand").

21. General Knowledge: Population

1. Over 53,000,000 (1965).

2. *Examples:* greater imports from world-wide trade; preservation of foods on journey to Britain (e.g. refrigeration, canning, gas-preserving); improvement of grain and vegetable cultivation resulting in greater yields per acre; chemical fertilizers; machines for sowing/harvesting; improved grades of cattle; battery-hens.

3. The most suitable population for the country's size and resources (sufficient to develop the country but not too many to be fed and cared for).

4. No, it has millions too many people for the size of the country and for what can be produced there.

5. No, too few people to develop the country fully and to protect it.

6. Nearly 12,000,000, which is less than a quarter of our present population.

7. Yes, there are approximately 2,000,000 more women than men.

8. Approximately 4,000,000 over the age of 70, the majority being women.

9. Approximately 25,000,000.

10. Approximately 17,000,000 men; 8,000,000 women.

11. The manufacturing industries.

12. Commerce (banking, insurance, trade, transport, etc.).

13. The United Kingdom could find work for a good many immigrants, but there is one important difficulty and this is the shortage of housing. We have not yet made adequate provision for our existing population.

14. To Australia (Canada and New Zealand are next).

15. The workers have to produce more and they have to pay more in taxation to maintain the non-productive elderly people.

16. Yes.

17. *Examples:* Bulgaria, Greece, Sweden, Ceylon, Chile. Australia has only a few millions more.

18. *Examples:* mechanization of farms; better conditions and pay in factories, etc.; greater imports of food; bigger attractions of town life; wars opened up new experiences to country people while they served in the Forces; enormous amounts of land taken for houses, factories, roads.

19. A great many people have moved southwards because the area is too mountainous and remote to support large populations. It is often bleak and cold.

20. No, because we rely on imports for about 50 per cent of the food we eat.

21. *Examples:* welfare state (pensions, health services, etc.); medical research and progress; machines produce more goods in less time; higher standard of living.

22. The Food and Agriculture Organization of the United Nations (F.A.O.).

23. Yes.

24. Manufacturing and commercial.

25. Mainly because of our need to produce more goods for export, to increase our "invisible" exports and to increase our standard of living.

26. Northern Ireland.

27. In "good" times the figure is about $1\frac{1}{2}$ per cent to 2 per cent; in "bad" times it has risen to as much as 10 per cent in some industrial parts of the country. But even 1 per cent represents about 250,000 people out of work.

22. Careers in Commerce

The salaries given in this section are approximate figures, intended for comparison purposes only. Salaries will vary a great deal from area to area.

MAINLY FOR GIRLS

The Office Junior

1. (a) Sorting and delivering the incoming mail.

(b) Collecting letters and documents to be posted, entering each item in a postage book, sticking down envelopes and operating a franking machine.

(c) Making tea or coffee for the staff.

(d) General filing duties.

(e) Some office juniors are also expected to keep a simple record of small cash payments, in a petty-cash book.

(f) Other juniors also type, and operate an addressing machine, duplicator or photo-copying machine.

	London Area	Provinces
2. Weekly salary about	£5	£3

3. Since the office junior is usually an unskilled girl, it is not essential for her to have attained a high academic standard. Such a school-leaver will be trained, by her employers, for the particular duties required. Employers usually look for girls who are neat in appearance, polite, cheerful, who speak clearly and are prepared to tackle their duties conscientiously. A knowledge of typewriting is an advantage and may lead to early promotion.

4. The prospects for the average office junior will depend largely on the way in which she works and the size of the business in which she is employed. Many office juniors, who work conscientiously, progress to clerical work in Invoice Departments, Buying Offices, Accounts Departments, etc., while others learn to typewrite at evening classes or at day-release classes. Some, who are proficient mathematicians, are taught how to use comptometers, while others become receptionists or switchboard operators.

The Copy Typist

1. As the name implies, a copy typist types letters or business documents from a "copy". Many spend their working hours typing out invoices, statements, accounts, order forms, insurance documents or statistics. The straight copying of letters is dying out, due to the introduction of the photo-copying machine.

	London Area	Provinces
2. Weekly salary at 16	£5	£4
Weekly salary at 25	£8	£6

3. A good copy typist should be able to type accurately at not less than 35 words per minute and hold an R.S.A. certificate in typewriting at Stage I or Stage II level.

4. The average copy typist remains a copy typist permanently. Some, who are ambitious and have a sound knowledge of English, go to evening classes or day-release classes to learn shorthand and so qualify as shorthand-typists.

The Comptometer Operator

1. The comptometer operator uses her machine to make arithmetical calculations. She will often work in an office or accounts department, making calculations for members of the staff or checking incoming and outgoing invoices and accounts for arithmetical errors.

	London Area	Provinces
2. Weekly salary at 16	£7	£4
Weekly salary at 25	£12	£9

3. Although not essential, a G.C.E., C.S.E. or R.S.A. qualification in Mathematics or Arithmetic is desirable, after which one would have to attend a recognized comptometer school for training. Many firms arrange this for suitable employees and pay for their training.

4. A conscientious comptometer operator would, after some years' experience, be in a position to look for a post as supervisor of a comptometer "pool".

The Telephonist

1. Telephonists operate a telephone switchboard. They put incoming calls through to the extensions asked for and give people, on internal extensions, an outside line when they require it. Many telephonists are also employed by the G.P.O. in telephone exchanges.

	London Area	Provinces
2. Weekly salary at 16	£4	£3
Weekly salary at 25	£9	£8

3. Most telephonists, working on small switchboards, are trained within their company. Those on larger boards are trained at a G.P.O. school for telephonists, on behalf of their employers. No special qualifications are called for, other than patience and an ability to speak clearly.

4. There are few prospects of promotion for telephonists, although some become supervisors of large switchboards.

The Audio-typist

1. An audio-typist types out letters and other documents from dictation which has been recorded previously on a dictaphone.

	London Area	Provinces
2. Weekly salary at 16	£7	£5
Weekly salary at 25	£12	£9

3. An audio-typist needs to be a highly proficient typist, preferably holding an R.S.A. Stage II certificate in typewriting.

135

She must also have a good command of the English language since she cannot expect any help from the machine with spelling and punctuation.

4. If an audio-typist has a good command of English, speaks clearly, dresses smartly, has a pleasing personality *and learns to write shorthand*, she can make a good personal secretary.

The Shorthand-typist

1. A shorthand-typist often works in a "pool" of shorthand and copy typists. She will be required to take dictation from a number of people working within the organization. She then transcribes her notes, on the typewriter, and presents the letters, memoranda, etc., to the staff who dictated them for signature.

	London Area	Provinces
2. Weekly salary at 16	£7	£4
Weekly salary at 25	£12	£9

3. To become a shorthand-typist one must, above all, have a complete grasp of the English language, be able to spell and punctuate without hesitation. Good shorthand and typewriting ability is absolutely essential, with speeds of at least 80 words per minute shorthand and 40 words per minute typewriting.

4. If a shorthand-typist works well and impresses her superiors with her efficiency, speech, personality, grooming, courtesy, etc., she will stand a good chance of being promoted to a private secretarial position when a vacancy occurs.

The Private Secretary

1. A private secretary has a varied and most interesting job. She acts as personal assistant to her employer, sorting his mail and presenting it to him with the necessary files for his attention. The secretary will then take down her employer's replies to the day's mail, type them out and present the letters for signature. She will also act as her employer's receptionist, greeting visitors and looking after them while they are waiting to see him. She must also, politely but firmly, prevent unwanted callers from disturbing her employer unnecessarily.

A secretary will plan itineraries for her employer, when he is about to make journeys on business, obtain airline tickets and make hotel bookings on his behalf.

	London Area	Provinces
2. Weekly salary at 18	£12	£8
Weekly salary at 25	£16	£12

3. A secretary must have achieved a good general education with at least three passes in G.C.E. at O-level, including English Language. A foreign language is a desirable qualification for certain secretarial positions.

Good shorthand and typewriting speeds are essential. A minimum speed of 100 words per minute in shorthand and 50 words per minute in typewriting are required for most secretarial positions, and these should be supplemented with business experience accumulated over several years as a shorthand-typist.

4. There are opportunities for good secretaries to obtain more responsible positions and some eventually become heads of departments within their organization.

The Medical Secretary

1. The duties of a medical secretary are similar to those of the secretary except that she will work for a doctor or specialist. In addition to dealing with general correspondence, the medical secretary will prepare notes and case-histories of patients from her employer's dictation, noting symptoms, drugs prescribed, etc., and arranging the doctor's programme of appointments.

	London Area	Privinces
2. Weekly salary at 19	£13	£11
Weekly salary at 25	£18	£16

3. The qualifications are largely the same as those required by the personal secretary, but must also include a sound knowledge of medical terminology and their shorthand outlines.

4. A medical secretary would work initially for doctors in general practice or for members of a hospital staff. An ambitious secretary would then progress towards becoming a medical secretary to a specialist or consultant.

The Punch-machine Operator

1. The punch-machine operator, as the name implies, operates a machine which puts information onto a card by punching holes in it. These holes are, in fact, a code for use in mechanized accounts. She extracts information from invoices and other business documents and transfers it onto the cards in the form of punched holes. These cards can then be "read" and analysed, at very high speed, by accounting machines.

	London Area	Provinces
2. Weekly salary at 16	£5	£4
Weekly salary at 25	£10	£9

3. No previous experience is required.

4. The punch-machine operator's only prospects are to be transferred to other branches of mechanized accounts, such as tabulating or sorting.

MAINLY FOR BOYS

The Accountant

1. In addition to an ability to keep business records in the form of accounts, accountants are consulted when new businesses are set up, audit (verify for tax purposes) the accounts of large and small businesses, advise on all manner of financial problems and help to determine the profitability of a company or particular process.

2. The salary of a trainee would have to be agreed individually with his employer. It will be somewhere in the region of £5 per week.

A newly qualified chartered accountant, in the London area, would earn £23 a week. His salary would then rise in stages commensurate with his ability, drive and determination.

3. A boy or girl, wishing to become a chartered accountant, must serve an apprenticeship with a chartered accountant. This is known as "taking articles". A candidate must have passed O-level G.C.E. in six subjects at not more than two sittings. English Language and Mathematics are compulsory, but may have been passed at additional sittings. The period of training is normally five years, although those with particularly good qualifications can complete their training in three years.

4. Once qualified, there are opportunities for an accountant to be taken into partnership in a major practice or he may set up in private practice on his own, after gaining the necessary experience. Many chartered accountants, working for large concerns, become company directors.

The Clerical Officer: Civil Service

1. Clerical officers are employed in all branches of the Civil Service, including Inland Revenue, National Insurance, the Board of Trade and the Post Office Savings Bank, where they perform a variety of clerical functions.

	London Area	Provinces
2. Weekly salary at 16	£6	£5
Weekly salary at 25	£12	£11

3. To become a clerical officer one must have passed three subjects in G.C.E. at O-level, including English Language, or have passed the Civil Service's own entrance examination.

4. Opportunities exist for taking examinations leading to appointment as executive officer.

The Executive Officer: Civil Service

1. Executive officers generally undertake advanced or administrative work and are often responsible for the work of a section or office staff.

	London Area	Provinces
2. Weekly salary at 16	£8	£7
Weekly salary at 25	£15	£13

3. To become an executive officer you must have passed five subjects in G.C.E. examinations, including English Language, with two of the subjects at A-level, and satisfy a selection panel that you have the qualities required to become a good exectuive officer.

4. Opportunities exist for executive officers to become senior executive officers with a salary scale from £1200 p.a. to £2000 p.a.

Customs and Excise Officers

1. Customs officers ensure that regulations concerning the import and export of goods are complied with. They see that quotas are enforced, import duties paid and are largely responsible for the detection and prevention of smuggling.

Excise officers are concerned with the duties payable on spirits, tobacco, etc., which have been processed or produced within this country.

	London Area	Provinces
2. Weekly salary at 16	£6	£5
Weekly salary at 25	£15	£14

3. Boys wishing to become Customs or Excise officers must have passed five G.C.E. O-level subjects, including English and Mathematics.

4. It is possible for talented officers to rise to higher grades, carrying greater responsibilities and higher salaries.

The Company Secretary

1. A company secretary is concerned with the general financial arrangements of the company. He ensures that dividends are paid out, in accordance with the instructions of the Board of Directors, and is generally responsible for the efficiency of the clerical staff within the organization.

2. The company secretary's salary will vary according to the size of the company for which he works. His salary would not be less than £1500 per annum, and would usually be considerably higher.

3. Company secretaries will normally be qualified accountants —chartered or incorporated secretaries, chartered or certified accountants.

4. Outstanding company secretaries are sometimes invited to become directors of the company for which they work.

The Bank Clerk

1. Bank clerks perform clerical duties in connection with bank customers' accounts. They sort cheques, deal with legal and investment matters, transact business with customers at the counter, pay out money, take in cash and cheques, issue travellers cheques and foreign currency, etc.

	London Area	Provinces
2. Weekly salary at 16	£8	£7
Weekly salary at 25	£15	£14

3. To become a bank clerk one must have passed at least four G.C.E. subjects at O-level, including English Language and Mathematics. Bank clerks are encouraged to study for Institute of Bankers' examinations at evening classes or by correspondence course.

4. Several banks claim that one out of every five bank clerks is eventually promoted to the position of bank manager.

The Insurance Clerk

1. Insurance clerks perform general clerical duties, make calculations concerning insurance premiums, undertake claims work and investigation.

	London Area	Provinces
2. Weekly salary at 16	£8	£7
Weekly salary at 25	£15	£13

3. One requires to have passes in at least three G.C.E. examinations at O-level, including English and Mathematics.

4. Insurance is a most lucrative and secure business and prospects of reaching high positions are generally good.

141

MODEL ANSWERS IN THE STRUCTURE OF COMMERCE

T. W. COX, B.Com., A.C.I.S., Lecturer in Business Studies, Medway College of Technology.

R. LAWSON, T.D., B.A. (Admin.), A.C.C.S., A.M.B.I.M., Head of Department of Commerce and Administration, South Devon Technical College.

Although this book is not intended as a textbook on commerce, it will serve as an extremely useful complementary volume, providing guidance for commerce and business students in tackling examination questions. It gives indications of the length of the answer and the subject matter the examiner would expect, and of the scope of the syllabus.

PRACTICAL COMMERCE

J. B. KING, F.B.S.C., Head of Department, David Lister High School, Kingston-upon-Hull.

The close integration of commerce with everyday life makes it a most appropriate subject for the practical and interesting approach to teaching which is the keynote of modern education. Yet commercial education tends to lag behind in the field of educational advance and a number of text books, written many years ago in a somewhat formal style, are still in active use. 'Practical Commerce' applies a straightforward, up-to-date approach to the teaching of commerce. It has been specially written for students taking commerce in the new Certificate of Secondary Education examinations and its practical approach also makes preparation for Royal Society of Arts and General Certificate of Education examinations, which do not display a bias towards Economics, more interesting and purposeful. An appendix gives organization details for interesting class projects together with suggestions for individual topics to help C.S.E. students and others required to submit projects to their examiners.